ARIZONA STATE FAIR

™

BLUE RIBBON
RECIPES

**GOLDEN
WEST ☼
PUBLISHERS**

Front and back cover photos provided by:
    Coliseum and Exposition Center Board

For further information about placing Entries in upcoming State Fairs, call the Entries Department at 602-252-6771 extension 306, or write:
                    Arizona State Fair
                    Attn: Entry Department
                    P.O. Box 6728
                    1826 W. McDowell
                    Phoenix, AZ 85005

Printed in the United States of America

ISBN #1-885590-19-9

Golden West Publishers, Inc.
4113 N. Longview Ave.
Phoenix, AZ 85014, USA
(602) 265-4392

THE EARS HAVE IT!

Arizona State Fair

OCTOBER 17-NOVEMBER 8, 1998

Dear Reader:

Each year, Arizonans from every corner of the state bring to the Arizona State Fair many incredible examples of their culinary creativity. The Homemaking Arts Building displays these delicious pies, cakes, breads, cookies, canned foods, and more in their respective categories. When the difficult job of judging the many exceptional entries is completed, the creator of the best entry in each category takes home the coveted Arizona State Fair Blue Ribbon.

With this first volume, we're proud to present Blue Ribbon-winning recipes from dozens of recent State Fair Winners. We congratulate them on their accomplishments, and we thank each of them for their generosity in sharing these special recipes with all their neighbors in Arizona.

If you've never entered a State Fair competition, perhaps this book will inspire you to try your luck next year! In the meantime, we hope you and your family will enjoy making—and most of all, eating—these irresistible dishes.

Sincerely,

Gary D. Montgomery
Executive Director

FEATURING THE DISNEY FAIR!

1826 W. McDowell Road • PO Box 6728 • Phoenix, AZ 85005-6728
Phone 602-252-6771 • Fax 602-495-1302

March of Dimes
Birth Defects Foundation
Arizona Chapter
1616 East Indian School Rd., #200
Phoenix, Arizona 85016-8602
Telephone 602 266-9933
FAX 602 266-9793

for Healthier Babies

Dear Friend:

Thank you for purchasing the premier edition of *Arizona State Fair Blue Ribbon Recipes.* Certain proceeds will be used to support the Arizona Chapter March of Dimes Birth Defects Foundation.

Your contribution will be used to help create a future for healthier babies here in Arizona, through prenatal care education, medical and community services, and research. Among the services your generosity helps to support are:

- **The "Mom Mobile"** (Maternity Outreach Mobile), a rolling doctor's office with two examination rooms to serve families in poor rural and urban areas, and to provide immunizations to children in need.

- Several **"Baby Mobiles"** transport expectant mothers to medical and other service appointments.

- **Baby Arizona** cuts through red tape to give pregnant women immediate access to medical care and other service appointments statewide.

Our thanks to you—and the Arizona State Fair—for your "blue ribbon support" of the Campaign for Healthier Babies!

Sincerely,

Henry Saldaña
Executive Director
Arizona Chapter March of Dimes

P.S. **Remember, if you're planning to have a baby you should take 0.4 milligrams of folic acid every day. Be sure and start before you become pregnant, to help prevent neural tube defects like spina bifida. You'll find folic acid in most multivitamins, and in green leafy vegetables, beans, asparagus, citrus fruits and juices, whole grain foods and liver.**

Blue Ribbon Recipes
Table of Contents

— VOLUME 1 —

Blue Ribbon Recipe Contributors

(Continued next page)

(Blue Ribbon Recipe Contributors continued)

(Continued next page)

(Blue Ribbon Recipe Contributors continued)

8 — *Blue Ribbon Recipe Contributors*

CANNING RECIPES

(Continued on next page)

(***Canning Recipes*** continued from previous page)

CANNING INFORMATION

Use only standard canning jars (no chips or cracks) and lids designed to fit them. Always use new self-sealing lids. Wash jars in sudsy water and rinse thoroughly. Then, pour boiling water over the jars and let stand in hot water until ready to fill. Follow manufacturer's instructions for sterilizing flat metal self-sealing lids and metal screw bands.

For canning to be effective, you must have the proper combination of temperature and time. Be especially careful when canning low-acid foods (particularly vegetables and meats). A pressure canner must be used with low-acid foods. Carefully follow the manufacturer's instructions. When in doubt about how long to place in boiling water bath or pressure canner, consult manufacturer's instructions.

Sour Orange Marmalade

(Ornamental Orange)

John V. Back — Phoenix

6 to 8 sour oranges　　　　**1 Tbsp. salt**
1 1/3 cups sugar　　　　　　**2 boxes pectin**

Juice 6 sour oranges and save the juice. (Use 8 oranges if small.) Cover the orange rinds with cool water and add one rounded tablespoonful of salt. Let stand overnight. Drain and rinse. Cover orange rinds with cool water and bring to a boil. Drain immediately. Repeat these 2 steps 2 more times. Let cool and chop orange rinds. Mix chopped orange rinds and juice. Measure and add 1 1/3 cups sugar per cup of mixture. Bring to a boil and then let cool for 5 minutes. Add 2 boxes pectin and stir 5 minutes. Put in sterilized jelly jars while still hot and seal jars with sterilized lids. Process for 10 minutes in boiling water canner. Yields 4 to 5 half pint jars marmalade.

Editor's note: For more canning information see page 10.

I was a fighter pilot in the Air Force for 30 years and flew combat missions in each of the three wars of my age group, WWII, Korea and Vietnam. After retiring from the Air Force as Colonel, I was a department director for Maricopa County for 17 years.

In 1983 my wife of 37 years died suddenly of cancer. I was determined to stay in the same house and I had no interest in marriage. My three sons and their families gave me all the family love I needed. I started cooking for myself, and friends suggested that ornamental oranges could be used for lemon pies and marmalade. I sought out recipes and tried both. The lemon pies were considerably short of "Great", but the marmalade wasn't bad. Each year I changed the recipe slightly until I arrived at the mixture for 1992. I don't plan any other changes.

I play golf, I enjoy spectator sports, the theater and music, and I make marmalade.

Pineapple Jalapeño Jam

Rosemary Whittier — Glendale

2 cans (20 oz. ea.) crushed pineapple
2 Tbsp. lemon juice
7 1/2 cups sugar
1 tsp. butter or margarine
1 jar jalapeño slices
1 pkg. Certo® Fruit Pectin

Drain pineapple thoroughly. Put in large kettle and add lemon juice and sugar. Bring to a boil; add butter or margarine. Boil for 2 or 3 minutes until sugar is completely dissolved. Dice up jalapeño slices to equal about 4 finely chopped tablespoonfuls. (Use less or more jalapeño to suit your taste.) Add diced jalapeño to pineapple mixture and boil for 2 more minutes. Add fruit pectin and bring back to a boil. Boil for 2 or 3 minutes, stirring constantly. Fill hot sterilized jars to within 1/4 inch of top and cover with sterilized lids. Process in boiling water bath for 10 minutes. Yields 3 1/2 pints.

Editor's note: For more canning information see page 10.

Pickled Okra

Maureen T. Winfrey — Phoenix

Wash **okra** and trim stems. Do not cut flesh. In sterilized pint jars, place **1 1/2 Tbsp. dill seed.** Tightly pack okra in jars. Add **1 yellow chile, sliced** and **two medium cloves of garlic** to each jar. Add **1/2 cup vinegar** to each jar and fill to within 1/2 inch from rim of jar with water. Add sterilized lids and screw tightly. Process in boiling water bath for 20 minutes. Allow to cure for at least 1 month. The longer they cure, the better they become!

Editor's note: For more canning information see page 10.

Plum Jam

Nikki Beath — Cottonwood

4 lbs. plums
8 cups sugar
1/2 cup water
1 box Ball® Fruit Jell Pectin

Pit and finely chop plums. Measure 6 cups of prepared plums into large saucepan. Add 1/2 cup water, simmer mixture for 5 minutes. Add 1 box Ball Fruit Jell Pectin. Bring this mixture to a full rolling boil over high heat, stirring constantly. Add 8 cups of sugar, return to a full rolling boil, boil hard for 1 minute, stirring constantly. Remove pan from heat, skim foam if necessary. Carefully ladle jam into hot sterilized jars, one at a time. Fill to within 1/4" of the top, wipe rim of jars with clean hot cloth, (to ensure proper seal). Place sterilized lids and bands on jars, twist firmly. Process for 10 minutes in boiling water canner. Remove jars after processing, let cool 12-24 hours. Check seals. Store in cool, dark place for up to 1 year. Yields 6 to 8 pints jam.

Editor's note: For more canning information see page 10.

I won a blue ribbon in 1992 for my Chinese Plum Jam. Chinese plums are very small, about the size of a large cherry. So, there was a lot of work involved pitting and chopping, but it was worth it for the dark, rich, and tasty jam it made. You can use any variety of plums in this recipe — black, red, Chinese, whatever. I find I have great results with Ball Fruit Jell Pectin. Whether you're a beginner or an expert, jam is fun and easy to make. Your family will love it and jam also makes a great gift!

Dried Apples

Heather Lynne Bilodeau — Tempe

Wash **apples** & dry. If dried apples will be eaten at a later time, peel and core; for decorations, it is not necessary to peel or core. Slice apples evenly, about 1/4" to 1/2" thick. Soak slices in **Fruit Fresh**® (follow package directions) for 2-3 minutes and drain. Place slices in food dehydrator in a single layer on each tray. Dry for 1 to 2 days.

Strawberry Jelly

Cindy Blair — Phoenix

2 1/2 qts. frozen berries (no sugar)   **1/4 tsp. margarine**
4 1/2 cups sugar   **1 box fruit pectin**

Thaw and crush berries. Pour into jelly bag, let drip until dripping stops. Press gently, measure juice to equal 3 3/4 cups juice (up to 1/2 cup water can be added for exact measure). Place in an 8-quart pot.

Measure 4 1/2 cups sugar in separate bowl. Stir fruit pectin into juice. Add 1/4 tsp. margarine. Bring to full rolling boil, stirring constantly. Add sugar all at once. Return to full boil and boil one minute, stirring constantly. Remove from heat. Skim off foam.

Sterilize jars and lids. Fill jars quickly to within 1/8" of top, wipe rims, cover with flat lids and screw on bands tightly. Set jars in boiling water canner for 10 minutes. When cool check seals. Yields 4 to 5 half pints jelly.

Editor's note: For more canning information see page 10.

I first made jelly with my grandmother when I was about 12 years old. She and my aunts lived on farms and we spent summers canning all kinds of fruits and vegetables. More recently I've been involved as a 4-H leader of a food preservation group.

Lemon Jelly

Frances Boyer — Phoenix

4 or 5 pint jars or jelly glasses
  and lids
4 1/4 cups cane sugar
4 or more lemons

1 1/2 cups water
1 pouch or 1/2 bottle
  liquid fruit pectin

Grate the rind and squeeze the juice from lemons. Mix together **1 Tbsp. rind, 1/2 of the lemon juice** and **1 1/2 cups water.** Let stand 10 minutes.

Sterilize jelly jars and lids and keep hot until jelly is ready.

Stir the lemon liquid and strain through a cloth. Measure 2 cups of this liquid and put in a large saucepan. Add the sugar and mix well. Place saucepan over high heat, bring to a boil, stirring constantly. Immediately stir in the liquid pectin and bring to a full rolling boil and boil hard for 1 minute, stirring constantly.

Remove from heat; skim off the foam with a metal spoon. Then pour the jelly quickly into jars. Seal immediately with lids screwed on tight. Process in boiling water canner for 10 minutes.

Yields 4 half pint jars plus a small glass for immediate eating pleasure!

Editor's note: For more canning information see page 10.

I began to experiment with various ways to make lemon jelly several years ago. I had been making orange and grapefruit jellies with much success and began thinking about lemon, too.

My recipe is not too sweet and not too tart. A preference for one or the other can be changed by increasing or decreasing the lemon juice or by decreasing or increasing the water. Do not alter the sugar amount.

My family and friends enjoy these homemade treats and it's a great way to have vitamin C on toast, pancakes or waffles.

Dried Herbs

Jean Brill — Phoenix

Begin by purchasing herb plants that have been started locally, or seeds that have been produced locally. This makes your plants "Arizona" hardy.

Plant them in a sunny location, in loose, rich soil. Water them frequently. Some need protection from the summer sun —some from frost. Feed with a good general fertilizer. Be sure to keep any fertilizers or pest killers off your plants.

Test to see if your herbs are more pungent in the early morning or at night. Cut them when they are at their most fragrant time of day. Trim herbs often to keep them from becoming "leggy" or "woody". Wash the plants with a hose the day before cutting.

When cutting herbs for drying, cut a good length of stem, tie the ends together in bundles, and hang them upside down in cool, dry air where they will not gather dust.

When the leaves and stems are fully dry and break easily, pull the leaves individually from the stems and store them whole in plastic bags or glass jars. Crush the leaves at time of using them.

Many herbs are available for a wide range of uses. If the nursery you use does not have what you want, ask them to order it for you. Most will do this.

I grow herbs for three uses, cooking (culinary), potpourri, and medicinal.

Canned Asparagus

Donna Brooks — Mesa

2 1/4 to 4 1/2 lbs. asparagus
1/2 tsp. salt to each pint or 1 tsp.
to each quart

Quantity to yield 1 quart—2 1/4 to 4 1/2 lbs asparagus. Wash and cut off scales (bracts.) Cut stalks into lengths 3/4" shorter than jar, or cut into 1" to 2" pieces. Blanch in boiling water for 1 to 3 minutes to wilt, then plunge into cold ice water until cool enough to handle. For whole pack, gather a bundle of stalks with cut ends down and pack (not too tightly) into sterilized jars; or fill to neck of jars with cut pieces. Add salt; then add boiling cooking liquid or water to cover asparagus leaving 1/2" head space. Apply sterilized lid and ring band. Processing time at 10 lbs. pressure: pints, 28 minutes—quarts 32 minutes.

Editor's note: For more canning information see page 10.

This was my first time canning vegetables. And the first time entering anything in the Fair. My husband, Wade, was the one who suggested I enter my canned goods in the Fair. I was reluctant but went ahead and entered. Was I ever shocked when I saw that blue ribbon and even more shocked that I had won a rosette. I cried so hard and have never felt more proud than on that day. It's a day I will never forget. I want to thank the Arizona State Fair for giving me such a wonderful memory. And a special thank you to my family for all their love and support. My husband, Wade, and girls, Sarah, Margaret and Dedra—the people who I do all my canning for.

Fig Jam

Tricia Brown — Phoenix

4 cups fig pulp
3/4 cup water
3/4 cup lemon juice

7 cups sugar
2 pkg. pectin

Stir together pulp, lemon juice and water. Add pectin until thoroughly dissolved. Bring to a boil and then add sugar slowly. Continue stirring, bring to a full rolling boil and continue for 5 minutes. Remove from heat and pour into sterilized jars. Fill to within 1/4" of the top, wipe rim of jar with clean hot cloth to ensure proper seal. Place sterilized lids and bands on jars and twist firmly. Process for 10 minutes in boiling water bath. Yields 4 to 5 half pint jars.

Editor's note: For more canning information see page 10.

My grandfather and I used to pick figs when I was young and I always remembered him making jam afterwards. About 2 maybe 3 years ago I asked him to teach me and every year since I have made it for home, the Arizona State Fair and gifts.

Canned Blueberries

Betty J. Burk — Taylor

Use **fresh blueberries** that have very gently washed, stemmed and picked over, to eliminate any bruised berries. Place berries in hot sterilized jars, leaving 1/2 inch head space. Pour prepared hot syrup to cover berries, adjust sterilized lids and process in boiling water bath for 10 minutes (pints) or 15 minutes (quarts). I use a medium syrup mixture: **3 cups sugar to 4 cups water**, bring to a boil, and boil for approximately 5 minutes until sugar is completely dissolved.

Editor's note: For more canning information see page 10.

Chile Salsa

Anthony Burns — Phoenix

10 fresh green chiles (New Mexican or Anaheim)	1 medium onion
	1 bunch green onions
4 large tomatoes	3 to 4 cloves fresh garlic
3 jalapeño peppers	cilantro
cumin powder	salt

Roast green chiles on barbecue or gas stove flame until skin is completely browned. Allow to cool under wet cloth or in a wet paper bag. Roast the tomatoes in the same fashion. While the chiles and tomatoes are cooling, combine remaining ingredients in a large bowl (not aluminum) as you process them. Garlic: peel and mince. Cilantro: chop enough to yield approximately 3 Tbsp. Onions: chop as fine as possible. Jalapeño peppers: remove stems and seeds and mince as fine as possible. Green chiles and tomatoes: remove skins under running water; remove stems from chiles; dice both and add cumin powder; stir gently to blend all ingredients. Salt to taste. Allow mixture to stand at room temperature 10 to 20 minutes before serving or refrigerating.

This recipe is for fresh use. To process for canning this recipe must be pressure canned due to lack of natural acidic qualities. Boiling bath canning methods are not sufficient.

Roasting chiles is time consuming. Consider roasting extra and freezing them in small bags for later use. The skin can remain and will peel easily under running water as they thaw.

Editor's note: For more canning information see page 10.

This chile salsa recipe is the result of four years of many canning attempts. It is not easy to correctly can this type of product without a vinegar taste. This was my first entry in the Salsa category.

I am a native Arizonan and credit my parents, who were Ohio refugees, with fueling my desire to find the best hot sauces and salsas. We visited many small Arizona restaurants and tamale shops in our search.

Back House Pickles

Susan R. Close — Phoenix

7 lbs. pickling cucumbers cut 1/4" thick
2 cups lime
2 gallons water

In large kettle, soak cucumber slices in lime and water mixture for 24 hours. Wash several times, rinse and cover with cold water. Soak 3 more hours; then drain. Add:

4 1/2 lbs. sugar
2 qts. cider vinegar
2 tsp. celery seed

2 tsp. whole cloves
2 tsp. mixed pickling spice
3 Tbsp. coarse salt

Let stand overnight. Put on stove and boil 35 minutes. Pack in sterilized, hot jars and seal with hot sterilized lids. Process in boiling water bath for 15 minutes.

Editor's note: For more canning information see page 10.

This is an old Roorda family recipe that I learned from them and have taught my daughters to make.

Orange Jelly

Patti Contreras — Stanfield

3 1/2 cups sugar
1 cup water
3 Tbsp. lemon juice

1/2 bottle liquid pectin
1 can (6 oz.) frozen, orange juice concentrate

In a large saucepan stir sugar into water and place on high heat. Stir constantly and bring to a full rolling boil that cannot be stirred down. Add lemon juice and boil hard for 1 minute. Remove from heat and stir in pectin. Add thawed orange juice and mix well. Pour jelly into hot sterilized jelly jars and seal with sterilized lids. Process in boiling water canner for 10 minutes.

Editor's note: For more canning information see page 10.

Pickled Figs

Dorothy M. Crotts — Phoenix

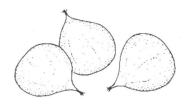

5 qts. firm ripe figs
1 cup baking soda
4 to 5 cups sugar
2 1/2 cups vinegar
1 Tbsp. salt
1 1/4 tsp. ground nutmeg
2 Tbsp. whole cloves
2 Tbsp. whole allspice
1 tsp. grated gingerroot
3 sticks of cinnamon

Wash and split the figs. Place in large bowl and sprinkle with the baking soda. Add 6 quarts of boiling water or enough to cover the figs. Let stand 5 minutes; well rinse in cool water and drain.

Bring 2 1/2 cups sugar and 2 quarts of water to boil in a large kettle. Add the figs and cook for 30 minutes or until tender. Add remaining sugar, vinegar, salt, nutmeg and the whole spices (tied in a cheesecloth bag). Cook until figs are clear. Let stand in a cool place overnight. Remove figs from liquid and pack in sterilized pint jars allowing 1/2" head space. Bring syrup to a boil and pour over figs. Place sterilized lids on jars and screw on tight. Process for 15 minutes in boiling water bath. Let cool.

Editor's note: For more canning information see page 10.

MaryAnn's Perfect Piccalilli

MaryAnn Gazdzik — Scottsdale

1 quart chopped cabbage
1 quart chopped green tomatoes
2 sweet red peppers, chopped
2 sweet green peppers, chopped
2 large onions, chopped
1/4 cup salt
1 1/2 cups vinegar
2 cups firmly packed brown sugar
1 1/2 cups water
1 tsp. turmeric
1 tsp. dry mustard
1 tsp. celery seed

In a large bowl combine cabbage, tomatoes, red and green peppers and onions. Mix with salt and let stand overnight. Next morning drain and press to remove as much liquid as possible. In a large saucepan, boil vinegar, water, sugar and spices for 5 minutes. Add the chopped vegetable mixture and bring to a boil. Pour into sterilized pint jars to within 1/2 inch of top. Wash and scald lids. Place lid on each and screw cap on tight. Process in boiling water bath for about 10 minutes. Makes about 4 pints.

Editor's note: For more canning information see page 10.

This recipe takes a little bit of time and effort, but it's worth it. . . and it's great on hot dogs!

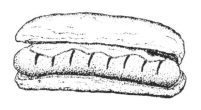

Light Grapes

Mary L. Andrews — Buckeye

For canned grapes, choose freshly picked **grapes,** none with dark stem ends. Use light syrup—**1 cup sugar** to **3 cups water** boiled for 5 minutes. Choose large similar sized grapes such as Thompson seedless. Wash and pick from stems. Pack grapes individually by hand, placing them in a circle around bottom of jar and place four grapes in center of circle. Repeat same procedure for all layers, making sure stem end is pointing down. Leave 1/2" head space and fill jar with boiling syrup covering grapes. Screw sterilized lid on jar firmly tight. Place in boiling water bath and process 20 minutes.

Note: If you want your canned fruit to keep that fresh look and taste, always use pure cane sugar. Beet sugar will cause discoloration and a winey taste after a few months.

Editor's note: For more canning information see page 10.

Pineapple Butter

Giuli Doyle — Phoenix

Clean **2 fresh pineapples** (the pineapples must be perfectly fresh or this recipe will not work. Remove all of the inner core and all of the outer skin. Use only the fruity part of the pineapples. Purée the pineapples until they become fluffy and white. Put the puréed pineapple in a large stock pot and add **brown sugar** and regular **granulated sugar** to taste. (Brown sugar should be two parts to one part of granulated sugar.) Add about **1/4 to 1/3 cup lemon juice** and cook until thick (as the pineapple cooks with the sugar it will be come a dark orange or nice brown color). Pour hot, into hot jars leaving 1/4" head space. Adjust caps. Process 10 minutes in boiling water bath. Yields about 4 to 5 pints.

Editor's note: For more canning information see page 10.

I do not use any spices in my jams or butters. If the fruit is perfectly fresh, no spices are needed.

Cherry Jam

Janet Henry — Scottsdale

4 cups (2 1/2 to 3 lbs.) pitted & chopped Bing cherries
1/4 tsp. salt
1/4 tsp. ground cinnamon
1/2 tsp. ground cloves
4 1/2 cups granulated sugar
1 pkg. powdered pectin
1/4 cup lemon juice
1/4 cup plus 2 Tbsp. DiSaronno®
  Amaretto
1/4 tsp. ground allspice
1 tsp. vanilla

In a 4-6 quart kettle, mix all ingredients except the sugar and 2 Tbsp. DiSaronno Amaretto. Bring mixture to a full rolling boil. Immediately add the sugar. Bring to a boil and continue to boil for 2 minutes. Remove from heat, skim foam. Stir in 2 Tbsp. DiSaronno Amaretto. Pour hot, into hot sterilized jars leaving 1/4" head space. Adjust caps. Process 10 minutes in boiling water bath. Yields 5-6 pints.

Editor's note: For more canning information see page 10.

As a Victorian enthusiast, I love tradition. I consider canning to be a traditional experience for anyone who loves to cook. I've been canning for about 10 years and although it's not something that my parents practiced or taught me, I've decided to start this tradition with my generation. For me it's been an experience of trial and error—experimenting with tested recipes and modifying them to suit my taste.

I look forward to continuing this tradition and submitting entries in the Arizona State Fair.

Canned Apples

Charles Hoyt — Phoenix

Choose medium sized unblemished **apples.** Have fruit at room temperature. Wash and brush gently in room temperature water which has a few (2-3) drops of dish detergent in it. Thoroughly rinse at least twice with room temperature water.

Prepare a large bowl or tub to hold at least two quarts of water with one or two Tbsp. of Fruit Fresh® or similar oxidizing preventive. Cut apple in half, carefully remove core, stem and flower remnants. Peel half of apple and immediately place into citric acid solution. Repeat this process with 7, 8 or 9 apples depending upon size.

Canning Procedure #1. (Open Kettle.) In a large kettle stir 1 1/2 to 2 cups of sugar (depending on sweetness of apples) into 4 cups of boiling water (steaming) and continue stirring to dissolve. Then place apple halves in hot sugar water and bring to a slow, gentle boil (cover ajar, not tight) for approximately 8 to 12 minutes.

Have sterilized jars, lids and caps ready. Lay in apple halves alternating around and up the jar until 3/4 full. Gently add the clear liquid to top of fruit. Finish layering in apples leaving at least 1/2" head space. Fill jar with boiling water and skim bubbles. Place on lid and screw cap as tight as possible. Set jar on level surface covered with papers. Jar will "seal" with a snap or pop within 10 to 15 minutes. Repeat process for each jar. Do not try to use left over juice for next batch. Pour in container to drink or use in fruit jello.

Canning Procedure #2. (Pressure Cooker.) Have your cooker checked for proper rubber seals. Put in the required amount of water according to your cooker directions. Have sterilized jars, lids and caps ready. Be sure you have your jar "lifter" ready to remove jars and a place prepared to put jars once they have been processed.

After the apple halves are prepared and put in the citric acid

(Continued next page)

(*Canned Apples* continued from previous page)

solution, lay them piece by piece in jar until jar is 2/3 full. Add prepared syrup **(1 1/2 to 2 cups sugar to 4 cups of water)**. Syrup should be at room temperature. Lay in last few apple halves, then fill jar with liquid to 1/4" from brim. Place on lid and screw cap tightly. Put in pressure cooker and process according to directions.

When completed, let pressure release according to directions before removing lid and carefully removing jars. When jars are cool, wipe with clean moist cloth. Check screw cap.

I am a seventy-five year old product of the Midwest. My early years were spent on a highly diversified farm with an emphasis on hogs, poultry and dairy. Being the last child of a family of seven I learned to do a lot of everything, including canning.

I've exhibited at the Arizona State Fair in both the Agricultural and Domestic Arts Departments. Over the years, I've received first places on canned peaches, pears and many other agricultural products as well as many second and third places in other categories.

Blackberry Jam

Keith Hochhaus — Phoenix

4 cups ripe blackberries　　　**4 cups cane sugar**
1 Tbsp. lemon juice　　　　　　**1 pkg. fruit pectin**

Wash, drain, and dry blackberries as much as possible. Place in a large flat-bottomed steel or heavy enamel pan. Add sugar, lemon juice and fruit pectin. Bring to a rolling boil, stirring to dissolve all sugar. Reduce heat to slow boil, stirring occasionally to avoid scorching. Continue to cook until jam is thickened. Pour hot into hot sterilized glass jars. Add sterilized lids and process in boiling water canner for 10 minutes. Store at room temperature.

Editor's note: For more canning information see page 10.

Lani's Family Bread & Butter Pickles

Sarah Jepson — Phoenix

1 cup of pickling lime
2 gallons of water

Combine pickling lime and water. Soak cucumbers for 24 hours, rinse thoroughly and slice.

1 red pepper
1 yellow pepper
4 onions cut up
6 cups of cucumbers
several pearl onions
* green peppers optional (changes taste)

Slice vegetables. Layer pickles in container (not metal) with ice, then a layer of vegetables. Sprinkle lightly with Kosher salt. Continue layers ending with last layer of ice. Cover and chill for 3 hours.

In another pan, combine:

> **5 cups of vinegar**
> **4 cups of distilled water**

Add:

2 tsp. celery seed	**1 Tbsp. whole cloves**
2 tsp. mustard seed	**1/2 tsp. pepper**
1 1/2 tsp. turmeric	

Bring all to boiling point and add **5 1/2 cups sugar.** Heat until sugar is dissolved.

Drain and rinse vegetables and add to vinegar solution. Simmer for 5 minutes. Pack into sterilized canning jars leaving 1/2 inch space from top of jars. Adjust sterilized lids and process in boiling water bath for 15 minutes.

Editor's note: For more canning information see page 10.

Canned Cherries

Thomas E. Kelly, D.V.M. — Phoenix

Purchase **12 lbs. Bing cherries**. Wash and remove pits carefully. Fill sterilized glass quart jars to 1/2" of top. Shake down while filling jars. Cover with boiling syrup leaving 1/2" space at top. Put on sterilized lid, securing in place by tightening ring. Process jars in boiling water bath for 25 minutes. Remove jars and check seal.

Syrup is made by mixing **4 3/4 cups sugar with 6 1/2 cups water** and bringing to boil (you may need more than one batch of syrup). This recipe yields approximately 7 quarts.

Editor's note: For more canning information see page 10.

Spiced Apples

Beverly A. Larson — Scottsdale

6 cups sugar
1 2/3 cups cider vinegar
1 tsp. red food coloring
4 cinnamon sticks

2 tsp. whole cloves
4 lbs. (about 12 medium)
firm Delicious apples

In an eight to ten quart stainless steel or enamel pan mix sugar, vinegar, food coloring, cinnamon sticks and cloves. Bring to boil over medium heat then reduce heat and simmer, stirring often, for ten minutes.

Peel and core apples; then cut crosswise into 1/2" rings. Add to syrup and cook uncovered, turning occasionally, until apples are barely tender (approximately 6-8 minutes).

Lift from syrup with fork and evenly fill hot, sterilized wide-mouthed jars leaving 1/2" head space. Run narrow, non-metallic sterilized spatula between apples and side of jars to release air bubbles. Wipe rims clean, top with hot sterilized lids, screw bands on firmly. Process for 10 minutes in boiling water canner. Makes about 4 pints.

Editor's note: For more canning information see page 10.

Peach Pickles

Gayle Manoz — Phoenix

24 small, firm, ripe peaches
2 cups sugar
2 sticks cinnamon
1 Tbsp. whole allspice
1 Tbsp. whole cloves
1 piece gingerroot
3 cups vinegar
2 cups water
2 cups sugar

Cling peaches are best for pickling, but freestone peaches may be used. To prepare peaches: Dip in boiling water for 2 minutes, then drop into cold water, remove peels and slice. Tie spices in a cheesecloth bag. Add spice bag, 2 cups sugar and water to vinegar. Bring to a boil. Add peaches a few at a time and simmer until heated thoroughly. Carefully remove peaches. Repeat until all peaches have been heated. Pour boiling syrup over peaches; cover and let stand 3 to 4 hours.

Carefully remove peaches from syrup. Add 2 cups sugar to the syrup and heat to boiling. Pour over peaches; cover and let stand 12 to 18 hours in a cool place.

Pack peaches into hot sterilized jars, leaving 1/4 inch head space. Add remaining 2 cups sugar to syrup. Bring to boiling, pour over peaches, leaving 1/4 inch head space. Remove air bubbles. Adjust sterilized tops. Process in boiling water bath for 15 to 20 minutes.

Yields approximately 6 pints.

Editor's note: For more canning information see page 10.

McMillen's Peach Butter

Glenda McMillen — Phoenix

2 quarts peach pulp (about 18 medium peaches)
3 cups white sugar
1 cup firmly packed brown sugar
1 tsp. nutmeg
1 tsp. cinnamon
1 tsp. allspice
1/2 tsp. ginger

To prepare pulp: Wash, pit and chop fully ripened peaches; cook until soft, adding only enough water to prevent sticking. Press through a sieve or food mill. Measure pulp. Add sugars and spices; cook until thick, about 30 minutes. As mixture thickens, stir frequently to prevent sticking and scorching. Or, if you have the time, cook over very low heat for several hours, stirring occasionally. Pour hot into sterilized jars, leaving 1/4 inch head space. Add sterilized lids and process in boiling water bath for 10 minutes. Yields about 4 pints.

Editor's note: For more canning information see page 10.

My husband, David, and I do our canning together as a family project. This is our fourth year of canning. We've entered the Fair every year and won several 1st, 2nd and 3rd place ribbons each year.

Peach Pit Jelly

Muriel Miller — Overgaard

After peeling and pitting peaches for canning or serving fresh, put peelings and pits (about 3 cups) in pan with water to cover well. Bring to boil, lower heat and simmer about 30 minutes. Drain. Strain juice through cheesecloth or jelly bag.

If you don't want to make jelly right after canning, place peelings and pits in plastic bag and drop in freezer till ready or prepare juice (using Fruit Fresh® to keep from discoloring) and freeze till another day.

1 box powdered pectin
2 1/2 cups peach juice
3 1/2 cups sugar

Mix pectin and juice in 4-6 quart kettle and bring to hard boil. Add sugar all at once, stirring gently. Bring to rolling boil, stirring constantly; boil for 1 minute. Remove from heat, skim foam. Pour into sterilized jars, leaving 1/4 inch head space. Clean sealing edge with damp paper towel. Place scalded lid and band on firmly tight. Process 5 minutes in boiling water bath. Yields 3 (8 oz.) jars.

Editor's note: For more canning information see page 10.

My mother, who never wasted anything, passed this recipe on to me.

Apple Cinnamon Jelly

Lisa Mousel — Lake Havasu City

2 3/4 cups apple juice
5 3/4 cups sugar
4-6 large cinnamon sticks (broken into pieces)
1 box fruit pectin
1/2 tsp. margarine or butter

Pour apple juice into 6 or 8 quart pot. Place sugar in a separate bowl; set aside. Into apple juice stir in fruit pectin, cinnamon sticks and margarine (to prevent foaming during cooking). Bring mixture to full rolling boil over high heat, stirring constantly. Quickly add sugar to juice and return to full rolling boil for 1 minute, stirring constantly. Remove from heat. Skim off any foam and remove cinnamon sticks. Pour into hot sterilized jars to 1/8 inch of top. Add sterilized lids and process in boiling water bath for 10 minutes. Yields 4 to 5 (1/2 pint) jars.

Editor's note: For more canning information see page 10.

Pepper Jelly

Jackie Mundy — Show Low

1 to 2 cups ground bell peppers (4 or 5 medium)
1/4 to 1/2 cup ground hot peppers (12 or more)
6 1/2 cups sugar
1 1/2 cups white vinegar
1 bottle Certo®

Mix all ingredients together except Certo. (Add hot peppers to taste.) Boil mixture 5 minutes, remove from heat, let stand 20 minutes. Add Certo and bring to a boil. Let boil 2 minutes. Pour into hot sterilized jars to 1/8 inch of top and add sterilized lids. Process in boiling water bath for 10 minutes. Yields 2 to 3 pint jars of jelly.

Editor's note: For more canning information see page 10.

Whiskey Grill Barbecue Sauce

Bruce F. Musall — Phoenix

8 cups worcestershire sauce
1 1/2 cups tomato juice
1/2 cup Tabasco® sauce
2 1/4 cups brown sugar
1/2 cup paprika
6 Tbsp. onion powder
4 cups apple cider vinegar

liquid smoke to taste
2 1/4 quarts ketchup
1/2 cup garlic, minced
2 cups sugar
1/2 cup salt
1/2 cup black pepper
1 cup Jack Daniel's®

Mix and simmer all ingredients except whiskey, for 1 hour. Add whiskey after mixture has cooked and cooled.

Makes 1 1/2 gallons sauce. Store in refrigerator until ready to use.

Russian Dills

Darlene McWhirter — Phoenix

3 cups sugar
3 cups dark vinegar

3 cups water
6 Tbsp. salt

Combine ingredients, bring to a boil and cool.

18 to 20 cucumbers
fresh dill
fresh garlic

onions (small or
    boiling size)
alum powder

Slice cucumbers lengthwise. Put in sterilized quart jars with cucumbers standing on end. Add to each jar a sprig of fresh dill, clove of garlic, small onion, and a pinch of alum powder. Pour in the sugar/vinegar syrup to within 1/4 inch of top. Put sterilized lids loosely on jars and place on cookie sheet. Heat in 300° oven for 15 minutes, then 200° for 25 minutes. Remove from oven and seal lids. Cool. Makes 4-5 quarts.

Editor's note: For more canning information see page 10.

Salt Brine Black Olives

Alana Thompson-Parrent — Chandler

2 qts. water
2 qts. vinegar (4 to 6% acidity)
1/4 cup salt
optional garnishes:
  celery, capers, jalapeños

1/8 cup sugar
4 Tbsp. olive oil
1 clove garlic
oregano

Pick ripe cherry-red to purple-black **olives** that are firm and unblemished. Start curing within 24 hours. Wash olives thoroughly in cool water. Sort according to size and color. Slash each olive twice, so brine solution can penetrate to remove the bitterness.

Fill one-gallon jars 3/4 full with olives and cover with brine solution of **1 1/4 cups of pickling salt** added to **1 gallon of water.** Use soft water for best results. Leave head space of 2 inches. Keep olives submerged in brine by weighing them down with a small, heavy block of wood, to prevent the top layer of olives from being exposed to the air and spoiling. The first couple of weeks is a period of active fermentation. To prevent pressure from building; leave jars uncovered, rest the lids on top, or use a paper towel held with a rubber band around mouth of jar. Stir olives every day and change brine as required (every 3 to 6 days) using the same solution strength.

Mold may develop, skim mold, drain solution and discard any spoiled olives. Rinse olives thoroughly in cool water and place in clean container. Replace solution.

When olives are no longer bitter to the taste (could take up to three months), rinse them in cool water. Fill 1-quart sterilized canning jars with 1 garlic clove, oregano, olive oil, olives and garnishes. Mix solution of water, vinegar and salt in a gallon container and pour over olives. Leave 1-inch head space. Screw sterilized lids on tightly and store in cool, dark place for up to one year.

Pineapple-Strawberry Jelly

Louise Fuller Pepper — Phoenix

1 cup fresh pineapple cut into
   1/2 inch pieces
4 1/4 cups sliced fresh strawberries
1/4 to 1/2 cup lemon juice
1 pkg. MCP® Pectin
8 1/2 cups sugar
1/4 tsp. margarine
5 to 6 pint jars and lids

Measure prepared fruit and lemon juice into a 6 to 8 quart saucepan. Measure sugar into a separate bowl. Set aside. Add 1 box of MCP pectin to fruit. Mix thoroughly.

Place fruit mixture over high heat. Bring to a full rolling boil (a boil that does not stop when stirred). Stir constantly to prevent scorching. (If mixture starts to scorch, reduce heat to medium.)

Stir in the sugar, mixing well. Bring to a full rolling boil stirring constantly. Continue to boil 4 minutes. Margarine can be added at this time to minimize foaming. Remove from heat. Skim off any foam.

Fill hot sterilized jars quickly to 1/8 inch from top. Wipe off rims. Cover with sterilized flat lids and screw bands on tightly. Process in boiling water bath for 10 minutes.

Editor's note: For more canning information see page 10.

Spiced Peaches

Carol J. Poteet — Gilbert

5 cups brown sugar
2 cups white vinegar
2 cinnamon sticks
2 Tbsp. whole cloves

4 qts. peaches, peeled,
   pitted and cut in half
1 cup peach brandy
   (secret ingredient)

Cook sugar, vinegar, spices and peach brandy 20 minutes. Drop in peach halves a few at a time and cook until tender. Pack into hot, sterilized jars adding syrup to 1/2 inch of top. Add sterilized lids and process in boiling water bath for 20 minutes.

Editor's note: For more canning information see page 10.

I was born 10-8-35 in St. Joseph, Missouri (Home of the Pony Express!!) I lived all my life there until June of 1993. We have children and grandchildren in the Phoenix area.

My first canning experiences were on my grandmother's farm in Maysville, Missouri (Maude Leddy Zug). She was one of nine children whose family came by covered wagon from Ohio to settle in that area.

Wild Grape Jelly

Bethel L. Winkle — Clifton

Start with **5 gallons** of both **ripe and unripe wild grapes** washed and stemmed. Crush grapes and add **1/4 cup water.** Heat to boil and simmer 10 to 15 minutes. Strain through jelly bag (to prevent crystals in jelly). Let juice stand overnight and strain juice again in the morning.

Heat 4 cups of grape juice and add **3 cups of sugar.** Stir until sugar is dissolved. Cook until syrup sheets off spoon. Pour into hot sterilized jars leaving 1/4" head space. Add sterilized caps and process 5 minutes in boiling water bath. Yields approximately 4 pints of jelly.

Editor's note: For more canning information see page 10.

Skit's
Mustard Crock Pickles

Robert Rehak — Glendale

25 to 40 (4-5 inch) pickling cucumbers
8 small green tomatoes sliced in half
1 medium green bell pepper
1 bag pickling spices
1 lump alum (2 tsp.)
1 cup pickling salt
8 oz. dry mustard
1 cup sugar
1 gallon cider vinegar (labeled 5% acidity)

Wash the cucumbers and remove 1/2 inch from blossom end. Cut the bell peppers in halves or strips and remove seeds. Cut the tomatoes in halves. Place cucumbers, green peppers, pickling spices, alum and tomatoes in a clean, uncracked 6 gallon stoneware crock to within two inches of the top.

In a large container mix pickling salt, dry mustard, sugar and vinegar together until dissolved and pour into crock. Continue filling with vinegar solution until the pickles (and plate—see below) are covered by 1 inch.

Set a scalded plate slightly smaller than the diameter of the crock on top of the cucumbers. To keep the plate submerged, fill one or more scalded quart jars with water, seal tops and place on plate.

Cover crock with clean towel held in place with string or cord. Store crock in a cool area where temperature is between 70-75° and allow pickles to ferment 2-3 weeks or until color is even. Remove scum daily and wipe inside edge of crock near solution line with clean cloth. At the end of fermentation you may process the pickles in jars per standard methods or you may keep in covered bell jar with solution if you prefer to let them continue to develop a stronger taste. You may add "new"

(Continued on next page)

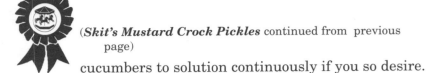

(**Skit's Mustard Crock Pickles** continued from previous page)

cucumbers to solution continuously if you so desire.

Check pickles for completed fermentation and wash before eating. Hang onto your taste buds and enjoy!

This recipe was given to me by my mother-in-law who told me that it was her mother's family recipe. She told me that she remembers her mother making these special pickles and that she looked forward to their unusual and tart taste. These pickles truly separate the strong from the weak in terms of "pucker power" levels.

Sweet Relish

Karen Laubinger — Mesa

1 quart chopped pickling cucumbers
2 cups chopped onions
1 cup chopped sweet green pepper
1 cup chopped sweet red pepper
1/4 cup canning salt
3 1/2 cups sugar
2 cups cider vinegar
1 Tbsp. celery seed
1 Tbsp. mustard seed

Sterilize 4 pint jars and lids. Combine cucumbers, onions, green and red peppers in a large bowl; sprinkle with salt and cover with cold water. Let stand two hours. Drain thoroughly; press out excess liquid. Combine sugar, vinegar and spices in a large sauce pot. Bring to boil. Add drained vegetables and simmer for ten minutes. Ladle hot relish into sterilized hot jars, leaving 1/4" head space. Wipe rim of jar and adjust lids. Process in boiling water bath for 10 minutes. Remove jars and place on wire racks to cool. Check seal in 1 hour. Allow to stand for 24 hours before storing.

Editor's note: For more canning information see page 10.

Cran-Peach Conserve

Lorilise Wood-Scarborough — Phoenix

2 lbs. cranberries, fresh or frozen
2 cups orange juice
6 lbs. peaches (fresh is best, but frozen works too)
    peeled, pitted and diced
10 cups sugar or 4 cups sugar substitute
1 1/2 Tbsp. lemon juice
1 Tbsp. brown sugar
2 packets of a preservative (I use Sure•Jell®)
20 oz. sliced almonds

In a large pot, mix cranberries with one cup of orange juice. Heat the mix on low, stirring occasionally. In another large pot, mix peaches with one cup orange juice; then add sugar, lemon juice and brown sugar, stirring frequently, and mashing the peaches at the same time. Heat this mixture on a medium setting.

When all the cranberries have "popped", bring to a boil, stirring constantly. Add cranberry mixture to peach mixture; add preservative, stirring constantly. When entire mixture is even in color and all fruit is soft, remove from heat. Stir in sliced almonds until they are coated in the juices.

Pour into hot sterilized jars to 1/2 inch from top and seal with sterilized lids. Process in boiling water bath for 10 minutes. Yields 6 (12 ounce) jars of conserve.

Editor's note: For more canning information see page 10.

I came up with this recipe as an alternative to the traditional cranberry sauce of our Thanksgiving dinner. Our Thanksgiving table includes family, lifelong friends, and many other invited guests. I was flattered by my blue ribbon from the Arizona State Fair for this entry, and equally so by the fact that last Thanksgiving we went through four jars of it at our extended family table.

Sweet Cucumber Pickles

Jill A. Smelter — Mesa

4 lbs. 4 to 5-inch pickling cucumbers
3 cup cider vinegar (labeled 5% acidity)
1 1/2 cups sugar
1 1/2 cups water
2 tsp. Kerr® Pickling Salt
2 tsp. mixed pickling spice
1 tsp. mustard seed
1 medium onion, sliced
(I add 1 small jalapeño pepper to each jar.)

Wash cucumbers and remove 1/16 inch from blossom end. Soak cucumbers overnight in cold water. Drain. Slice cucumbers into 1/4 inch slices. In a 6 to 8 qt. saucepan, combine vinegar, sugar, water, pickling salt, pickling spice and mustard seed. Bring to a boil over medium-high heat. Stir cucumbers into boiling vinegar mixture. Bring to a boil over medium-high heat until cucumbers lose bright green color, about 5 minutes, stirring occasionally. Immediately fill hot sterilized jars with cucumber mixture (I place a small jalapeõ in each jar before adding the mixture). Top mixture in each jar with 1 to 2 slices of onion, leaving 1/2 inch head space.

Carefully run a non-metallic sterilized utensil down the inside of the jars to remove trapped air bubbles. Wipe jar tops and threads clean. Place hot sterilized lids on jars and screw bands on firmly. Process quarts for 20 minutes and pints for 15 minutes in boiling water bath.

Yields 4 to 5 pints or approximately 2 quarts of cucumber pickles.

Editor's note: For more canning information see page 10.

I am originally from Kansas and did some home canning there on a small farm where I lived with my

(Continued on next page)

(*Sweet Cucumber Pickles* continued from previous page)

husband. *It was a nice little farm with peach and pear trees, a 25 quart a year strawberry garden, asparagus grove, blackberry vines, plus all the tomatoes, cucumbers, zucchini, corn, etc. that we planted.*

We eventually moved to Arizona and had 3 children. When they were old enough, I started teaching them to make jams and have moved them up to peaches and pickles. They also dabble in baked goods and crafts. This past year, it became a family thing when my husband entered his "Bread Machine Bread" in the County Fair.

Crosscut Pickle Slices

Linda Rowley — Tempe

4 qts. sliced cucumbers (approximately 6 lbs.)
1 1/2 cups (12-15 small) sliced white onions
2 large garlic cloves
1/2 cup salt
2 trays ice (crushed or cubes)
4 1/2 cups sugar (or less if desired)
1 1/2 tsp. turmeric
1 1/2 tsp. celery seed
2 Tbsp. mustard seed
3 cups white vinegar

Wash cucumbers. Cut off 1/2 inch of blossom end and discard. Slice (unpeeled) cucumbers into 1/8 to 1/4 inch slices. Place in a large bowl or crock and add onions, garlic and salt and mix thoroughly. Cover with ice and let stand for 3 hours. Drain thoroughly and remove garlic cloves. Combine sugar, spices, and vinegar in a large kettle and heat just to boiling. Add cucumbers and onions; heat for 5 minutes. Pack hot pickles loosely into sterilized hot pint jars to 1/2 inch from top and add sterilized lids. Process in boiling water bath for 5 minutes. Remove jars and check seals. Set jars upright to cool. Yields 7 pints.

Editor's note: For more canning information see page 10.

Spiced Figs

Martha F. Scott — Phoenix

Wash **5 lbs.** ripe but firm **figs** with stems. Without removing skins, cover the figs with **1 cup baking soda** and **1 gallon boiling water** and let figs set in soda solution 5 to 10 minutes. Remove fruit to cold water, drain and then mince thoroughly and gently.

1 1/2 cups water
6 1/4 cups sugar
2 or 3 sticks of cinnamon, crushed
1/3 cup whole cloves
1 1/2 cups vinegar

Bring sugar and water to a boil. Add spices and vinegar - stir until blended. Add figs to syrup and cook slowly on low for 1 hour. Pack in hot, sterilized jars. Cover with hot syrup and seal with sterilized lids. Process in boiling water bath for 20 minutes.

Editor's note: For more canning information see page 10.

This fig recipe was given to me by my mother, Mrs. Harold F. Hensley. My parents came to Phoenix for my mother's health in 1927. We lived in Sunnyslope until I was 9, then moved to 19th Avenue and Indian School where we had 10 acres of land. We had cows, horses, pigs, chickens, turkeys and fruit trees. We had white and black figs and dried and canned many of them. We also had all kinds of dates, some of which we ate and others that we sold for 10 cents a pound. We canned our own olives and all of the other kinds of fruits available to us.

Zucchini Relish

Mark Soto — Glendale

9 cups finely chopped zucchini (6 large)
1 1/2 cups finely chopped green bell pepper (1 large)
1 1/2 cups finely chopped red bell pepper (1 large)
3 cups finely chopped onions (4 large)
1/2 cup salt
3 1/2 cups sugar
3 cups vinegar
1 cup water
1 tsp. mustard seed
2 tsp. celery seed
2 tsp. turmeric
green food coloring

Soak vegetables with salt in water to cover for 3 hours. Scatter ice cubes on top. Rinse thoroughly and drain well. Boil together sugar, vinegar, 1 cup water and spices for 3 minutes. Add drained vegetable mixture to hot liquid, add 2 drops food color and boil for 10 minutes. Pour into hot sterilized jars leaving 1/2" head space. Add sterilized lids and process in boiling water bath for 10 minutes.

Editor's note: For more canning information see page 10.

Harvard Beets

Lorraine Sweeney — Phoenix

3/4 cup sugar
1/2 cup water
1/3 cup white vinegar
2 tsp. cornstarch

4 cups cooked beets, cubed
1/4 tsp. salt
1/4 tsp. pepper

Boil first four ingredients for 5 minutes. Add cooked beets, salt and pepper and simmer for 1/2 hour.

Fill sterilized jars to within 1/2 inch of top and seal with sterilized lids. Process in boiling water bath for 20 minutes.

Editor's note: For more canning information see page 10.

Canned Tomatoes

Otto Viertel — Phoenix

Use garden fresh **tomatoes**. Dip in boiling water for 30 seconds then quickly put in ice water. Remove skins and core. Cut tomatoes into quarters. Pack tightly in hot sterilized jars with 1/2 inch head space.

Add:

1/2 tsp. coarse salt per quart jar
2 Tbsp. lemon juice per quart jar

Cover with sterilized lids and process in boiling water bath for 45 minutes.

Editor's note: For more canning information see page 10.

Bread & Butter Pickles

Enid Steffens — Glendale

25 pickling cucumbers
8 medium onions
1/2 cup coarse salt
5 cups cider vinegar
2 to 4 Tbsp. pickling spice

5 cups sugar
2 Tbsp. mustard seed
2 tsp. turmeric
1/2 tsp. ground cloves

Scrub cucumbers and slice thin. Do not peel. Cut onions into thin slices and combine with cucumbers and salt. Let stand, covered, at room temperature for 3 hours. Drain well. Combine remaining ingredients in a large kettle and bring to a boil. Add drained cucumbers and onions and heat thoroughly but do not boil. Pack into hot sterilized pint jars, leaving 1/8 inch head space. Seal immediately with sterilized lids. Process 5 minutes in boiling water bath.

Editor's note: For more canning information see page 10.

In 1992 Enid was 70 years old. In the last few years she has gone back to school and received her GED.

Fruit Leather

Sherry Tucker — Avondale

5 cups ripe fruit   1/4 cup sugar   water

Clean, cut up and remove pits (if necessary) from the fruit. Place in microwave dish and stir in the sugar. If fruit is not very juicy, add a little water. Cover and microwave on high for 10 minutes. Remove and stir. Cover and again place in the microwave oven and microwave on high another 10 minutes. Remove, stir again, cover and microwave another 3-5 minutes or until the fruit is tender and juicy. (The fruit can also be cooked in a saucepan over a low heat, stirring occasionally to prevent burning.)

Remove from the microwave and ladle fruit into a blender. Blend the fruit until it becomes a sauce mixture. Pour the sauce into a colander and strain to remove remaining skin.

Pour 5 or 6 small circles, using 1/4 cup of sauce for each circle, on a cookie sheet that has been covered with securely taped plastic wrap.

My husband, Floyd, used wooden 2 x 4's to make a framework to sit on top of my outdoor table. I tack the tightly stretched cheesecloth to the top of the framework and place the cookie sheets underneath. Then I use clothespins to pin the excess cheesecloth to the table edge so that insects cannot get to the fruit. It works!

On a hot day with temperatures over 100° the fruit will dry in one day if the sauce is put out in the early morning. If it is still sticky to the touch and hard to peel off, store the cookie sheet, covered, overnight—then place outside for several hours more the next day.

Peel the dried fruit from the plastic wrap, roll up, then cover with plastic wrap. The dried fruit can be stored six weeks on the shelf, six months in the refrigerator, or indefinitely in the freezer.

(Continued next page)

(*Fruit Leather* continued from previous page)

I make up four batches (25 cups of fruit) at a time and use an 8 quart dish to cook it in. This way, I can make up the sauce ahead of time and store it in large sealed plastic containers which I freeze. Then, when the weather is dry and hot, I thaw the sauce in the refrigerator and dry the fruit.

The dried fruit has been a good way to use all the fruit from our trees and to get my kids to eat more of it. They take it to school and sporting activities to share with their friends.

Pears

Lesley Potter — Phoenix

Use **ripe pears**. Remove peel, core and cut into halves or quarters. If peeled fruit is to stand several minutes before canning, drop into a mild salt solution to prevent discoloration. Drain well.

Add **1 tsp. Fruit Fresh**® to the bottom of each hot sterilized quart jar. Pack raw pears to within 1/2 inch of top. Add boiling syrup also to within 1/2 inch of top. (I use medium syrup—see below.) Put on sterilized lid and screw band firmly tight. Process in boiling water bath: Quarts 30 minutes, pints 25 minutes.

Medium Syrup: **1 cup sugar** to **2 cups water.** Boil sugar and water together until sugar is dissolved. Keep hot but do not let it boil down. Syrup should be boiling when poured over fruit.

Editor's note: For more canning information see page 10.

Grandmother Wareham's Mustard Pickles

Myra J. White — Peoria

2 green peppers (optional)
2 red sweet peppers (optional)
3 pints (6 cups) pearl onions
2 quarts (8 cups) firm pickling cucumbers,
   (cut into chunks)
2 small heads of cauliflower (cut into florets)
1 1/2 cups coarse salt
cold water

If using peppers, remove seeds and cut into small strips. Peel onions, and wash and cut cucumbers; mix peppers, onions, cucumbers and florets together in a scalded crock or other large earthenware container. Sprinkle salt over all and add enough cold water to completely cover. Let stand overnight and then drain thoroughly.

Mustard Sauce

1 1/2 cups flour
3 1/4 cups sugar
3 Tbsp. turmeric
2 Tbsp. mustard seed

2 cups water
7 1/2 cups cider vinegar
3/4 cup dry mustard

Combine flour, sugar, turmeric and mustard seed in a large saucepan. Gradually add 2 cups water, stirring until smooth. Stir in vinegar and dry mustard. Cook until sauce coats spoon and mixture thickens, stirring constantly. Add vegetables and simmer for 15 minutes.

Pack immediately into sterilized jars, leaving 1/4 inch head space. Add sterilized caps and seal. Process jars 10 minutes in boiling water bath to ensure against spoilage.

Yields 8 to 9 (16 oz.) jars.

Note: The flavor of mustard pickles mellows with age.

(Continued on next page)

(*Grandmother Wareham's Mustard Pickles* continued from previous page)

Allow at least 1 or 2 months storage before using.

I don't use the peppers as I feel that they adversely affect the flavor. Also, the peppers may alter the color.

This recipe has been around since my grandmother was a child in England so it's been tried and tested for many years. I can remember eating the pickles, always on Sunday and especially on holidays. My mother says she can remember her mother making them on one day and then making a large amount of bread the next. My mother comes from a large "yours, mine and ours" type of family (there were 17 brothers and sisters) from Cape Breton, Canada so you can imagine how many jars of pickles she would do at a time. She would also "do up" corn, carrots, beets, beans and any other vegetable and fruit that was available.

The pickles taste best cold from the refrigerator with any kind of meat. I personally like the mustard sauce on ham sandwiches. I sometimes even make the sauce and can it just for that reason.

Chili Con Carne

Fred Santesteban — Chandler

Brown **1 lb. coarse grind, ground beef** (or grind cheap beef in food processor). Add **3 each; jalepeño peppers, hot Hungarian (yellow) peppers and large green peppers chopped** (seeds and membranes removed). Add **1/2 medium onion, coarsely chopped.** Add **1 tsp. chili powder, 1/2 tsp. each** of **cumin and cilantro (fresh).** Add **1 fresh tomato, chopped** (seeds removed). Add water to desired consistency.

Fill sterilized jars to 3/4" from top, seal with sterilized lids. Steam for 25 minutes at 10 lbs. pressure in pressure canner.

Editor's note: For more canning information see page 10.

CAKE RECIPES

Cherry Almond Delight

Elizabeth Brockway — Phoenix

2 1/4 cups sifted cake flour	1 1/2 cups sugar
3 tsp. baking powder	1 tsp. salt
2 eggs, separated	1/3 cup vegetable oil
1 cup milk	1 tsp. cherry extract
1 tsp. almond extract	

Preheat oven to 350°. Line two nine-inch cake pans with wax paper. Spray the wax paper with oil. Sift flour, 1 cup sugar, baking powder and salt into a large mixing bowl. In medium size mixing bowl, beat egg whites until foamy-white and doubled in volume. Very slowly sprinkle 1 tablespoon of sugar at a time from remaining 1/2 cup, beating constantly, until meringue forms soft peaks.

Blend vegetable oil and 1/2 cup milk into flour mixture and beat 2 minutes at medium speed. Stir in egg yolks, extracts and the remaining 1/2 cup milk; beat 1 minute.

Fold in meringue until no white streaks remain then pour evenly into prepared cake pans. Bake for 35 minutes or until tops spring back when lightly pressed with finger tips. Cool in pans on wire racks 5 minutes. Loosen sides with knife, invert onto racks and peel off wax paper. Cool completely.

Cherry Delight

1/2 cup sugar
4 Tbsp. all-purpose flour
1/4 tsp. salt
2 eggs, separated (reserve whites for frosting)
1 1/2 cups milk, scalded in large saucepan
1/2 cup chopped, toasted slivered almonds
1 tsp. each cherry and almond extracts
1/2 cup chopped maraschino cherries (reserve juice
    for frosting)
2 Tbsp. butter

In a medium size bowl combine sugar, flour, and salt. Beat egg yolks with a fork in a small bowl and stir in 1/2 cup of scalded

(Continued on next page)

*(**Cherry Delight** continued)*

milk. Then slowly stir mixture back into large sauce-pan of scalded milk. Stir in dry ingredients and cook over medium heat stirring constantly until mixture thickens and boils (about 1 minute). Remove from heat. Stir in remaining ingredients and cool completely.

Place one layer of cooled cake on serving platter. Spread all of the **Cherry Delight** on top of layer. Place second layer on top and frost.

Frosting

2 reserved egg whites
2 Tbsp. light corn syrup
1/2 tsp. cherry extract
1 pound box powdered sugar, sifted
1/4 tsp. cream of tartar
2 1/2 Tbsp. reserved maraschino cherry juice
1 1/2 tsp. almond extract

Combine egg whites and cream of tartar in a large size mixing bowl. Beat until egg whites form stiff peaks. Combine corn syrup, cherry juice and extracts in small bowl. Add alternately with powdered sugar to egg white mixture—beating well after each addition until frosting is creamy, stiff and easy to spread. Spread on sides and top of cake.

Devil's Dump
Chocolate Cake

Virginia Burke — Phoenix

1 stick butter	2 squares bitter chocolate
1 1/2 cups cake flour	1 tsp. baking powder
1 cup sugar	1 tsp. baking soda
1 cup buttermilk	2 eggs, beaten
1/2 tsp. salt	1 tsp. vanilla or Myer's® rum
1 cup chopped pecans	

Grease and flour two 8-inch pans. Preheat oven to 350°. Sift flour, baking powder and salt together. Add baking soda to buttermilk and stir well.

Melt butter and chocolate. Remove from heat. Add sugar to chocolate mixture and mix well. Add beaten eggs, mix well. Add buttermilk/baking soda mixture, mix well.

To this mixture slowly add flour mixture while stirring constantly. Finally, add vanilla (or rum) and nuts and mix well.

Pour into greased pans and bake at 350° for 25 minutes.

Coffee Frosting

1 square bitter chocolate
1 stick butter (softened)
1 box powdered sugar
4 Tbsp. cold coffee
pecans, chopped

Melt chocolate and let cool. Add softened (not melted) butter to chocolate along with 3-4 Tbsp. of cold coffee. Mix together.

Begin adding powdered sugar while continually stirring. Add powdered sugar until appropriate consistency is reached for frosting the cake.

Assemble cake and sprinkle chopped pecan nuts on top.

Dark Fruit Cake

John Eichhorn — Phoenix

2 cups flour
1 cup sugar
2 tsp. baking powder
1 tsp. baking soda
1/2 tsp. each cinnamon, nutmeg, cloves
1/4 tsp. salt
5 oz. chopped dates
1 cup brandy
1 egg, lightly beaten
1 Tbsp. vegetable oil
1 tsp. vanilla extract
2 lb. candied mixed fruit
1/2 lb. walnuts, coarsely chopped
1/2 lb. pecans, coarsely chopped
1 cup dark raisins
1 cup golden raisins

Prepare three 4 x 8 bread pans by lining the bottoms with waxed paper and spraying with oil. Preheat oven to 325°.

Sift together dry ingredients and add dates. Mix candied fruit, nuts, and raisins in a very large bowl. Stir in the flour mixture and then the liquids. Batter will be very stiff.

Press batter into pans and place on middle rack of oven. Put a pan of water on the bottom rack. Bake at 325° for 50 to 60 minutes or until the tops are browned. Remove from oven and loosen edges with a knife. Cool on a wire rack for 15 minutes; then remove from pans.

Loaves may be glazed with hot corn syrup and decorated with pecan halves and candied cherries, if desired.

Arizona State Fair
Cheesecake

Bill Graves — Mesa

2 cups finely crushed graham crackers
1 1/2 tsp. cinnamon
1/3 cup sugar
1/4 pound butter, melted (1 stick)

Butter a springform pan liberally. In a small bowl combine all ingredients. Line pan firmly with crumb mixture, covering bottom and up the sides to about 2". Crumbs should be about 1/4" thick. Put in freezer to chill, or into oven and bake for 10 minutes at 350°. Both ways work. Set aside.

2 pkgs. (8 oz. each) cream cheese, softened
1 cup sugar
1 tsp. vanilla
1 ctn. (16 oz.) sour cream
4 eggs

In a large mixer bowl combine the first 4 ingredients. Add eggs and beat on medium speed until mixture is blended and smooth.

Pour into graham crust and bake at 350° for 40 minutes. Then turn oven off. Let cheesecake stay in oven for 1 1/2 to 2 hours. Do not open door.

8 oz. cream cheese, softened   **1/3 cup sour cream**
1 tsp. vanilla   **2 Tbsp. sugar**
1 small can of crushed
**   pineapple, drained well**

In a small mixer bowl, combine ingredients and whip at high speed for 5 minutes. Spread on top of cooled cake. Decorate with a slice of pineapple and fresh raspberries.

Keep cheesecake refrigerated; it is best after 2nd day.

(Continued on next page)

My cooking life began 71 years ago in the old stagecoach tavern my mother owned and operated in Hampton Falls, New Hampshire. Inns and hotels were in vogue for the traveling guest as it was before the days of motels.

My first fascination with cooking began as a small boy of 3 years when my grandmother would set me on the counter near her while she prepared and baked exciting delights for our guests. Of course, the batter spoon and bowl were mine.

Those days vanished into time as did the inn but from that day to this I have loved baking. I never enjoyed the everyday life of preparing the daily meals. I leave that to my wife. I enjoy polishing the meal with some special delight that brings Oooo's and Ahh's from our friends and family. My best wishes to the folks who try this recipe. I hope you will enjoy it!

Carrot Cake

Kathleen Addie — Phoenix

4 eggs	2 cups flour
1/2 cup salad oil	1 tsp. cinnamon
2 cups sugar	1/2 tsp. salt
3 grated carrots	1 tsp. vanilla
1 cup chopped nuts	2 tsp. baking soda

Beat eggs, add oil, sugar and then dry ingredients. Add carrots and nuts. Pour into a 9 x 13 cake pan and bake 45 minutes at 350°.

Frosting

1/4 lb. butter or margarine	1 (8 oz.) pkg. cream
1 lb. powdered sugar	cheese (softened)

Beat ingredients together and spread on cake when cool.

German Chocolate Cake

Judy Huyett — Phoenix

1 pkg. (4 oz.) Baker's® German Sweet Chocolate
1 cup butter
2 cups sugar
4 eggs, separated
1 tsp. vanilla
2 1/2 cups sifted cake flour
1 tsp. baking soda
1 cup buttermilk
1/2 cup boiling water
1/2 tsp. salt

Melt chocolate in boiling water and then cool. Cream butter and sugar until fluffy. Add egg yolks, one at a time, beating well after each. Blend in vanilla and chocolate. Mix flour, soda and salt. Add flour mixture, alternately with buttermilk, to chocolate mixture, beating after each addition until smooth. Fold in stiffly beaten egg whites. Pour into three 8" layer pans lined on bottoms with waxed paper. Bake at 350° for 30-35 minutes. Cool. Frost tops only with *Coconut-Pecan Frosting.*

Coconut-Pecan Frosting

Combine **1 cup evaporated milk, 1 cup sugar, 3 slightly beaten egg yolks, 1/2 cup butter** and **1 tsp. vanilla.** Cook and stir over medium heat until thickened (about 12 minutes). Add **1 1/3 cups Baker's® Angel Flake Coconut** and **1 cup chopped pecans.** Cool until thick enough to spread, heating occasionally. Enjoy!

German Chocolate Cake with Baileys® Irish Cream

Anne Justice — Phoenix

2 cups sugar
1 cup shortening
7 eggs, separated (reserve 3 yolks for filling)
1 cup buttermilk
1 tsp. soda
2 1/2 cups flour
1 pkg. German sweet chocolate
1 tsp. vanilla
1/2 tsp. salt
1 (50 ml) bottle of Baileys® Irish Cream

Dissolve chocolate in 1/2 cup boiling water. Cream shortening with sugar. Add beaten egg yolks, then 3/4 cup of buttermilk, alternate with flour. Dissolve soda in 1/4 cup buttermilk. Add chocolate mixture. Fold in 7 stiffly beaten egg whites and add vanilla. Add Baileys Irish Cream and stir.

Pour into three 9-inch cake pans that have been lined with wax paper. Bake at 350° for 25-35 minutes or till done. Cool before removing from pans.

Filling

1 large can Carnation®
  Evaporated Milk
1 1/2 cups sugar
1 stick butter
3 egg yolks

1 cup coconut
1/2 cup pecans
1 tsp. vanilla
1 Tbsp. Baileys® Irish
  Cream (optional)

Place first four ingredients in a double boiler. Mix and cook until slightly thick. Add vanilla and cool. Add coconut, pecans and Baileys. Filling should be yellow and look like it will run off the cake—but it won't.

Chocolate Roll

Darlene Karolyi — Phoenix

1 cup SoftaSilk® Cake Flour
1 tsp. baking powder
3 eggs
1/3 cup water
1/4 cup Hershey'®s European
Style Cocoa
1/4 tsp. salt
1 cup sugar
1 tsp. vanilla

Heat oven to 375°. Line jelly roll pan 15 1/2 x 10 1/2 x 1 with wax paper and grease the wax paper.

In medium bowl stir together cake flour, cocoa, baking powder, salt. Set aside. In a small bowl, beat eggs 5 minutes with electric mixer. Pour eggs into large bowl and gradually beat in sugar on low speed. Blend in water and vanilla gradually. Add flour mixture beating just until batter is smooth. Pour into pan spreading to corners. Bake 12-15 minutes or until toothpick in center comes out clean. Loosen cake at edges of pan, invert on towel and sprinkle with cocoa. Carefully remove paper; trim off hard edges. Now, while hot, roll cake in towel from narrow side and cool on wire rack. When cool, unroll and fill with ***Chocolate Whipped Cream Filling.*** Roll up without towel. Glaze with ***Chocolate Glaze.***

Chocolate Whipped Cream Filling

1/2 cup of sweetened Baker's® Whipping Cream
1 Tbsp. powdered sugar
1 Tbsp. Hershey'®s European Style Cocoa

Chill a deep, narrow mixing bowl and beaters in freezer. Place all ingredients in bowl and beat on high speed about 5 minutes. Be quick so the bowl won't loose its chill. Now unroll cake. Spread filling and roll up again. Place on plate with seam side down and glaze with ***Chocolate Glaze.***

(Continued on next page)

(*Chocolate Roll* continued)

Chocolate Glaze

1/4 cup Land-O-Lakes® Butter
1 tsp. vanilla
1 oz. Nestlé® Pre-Melted Cocoa Bake
1 cup powdered sugar
2 to 3 Tbsp. hot water

Melt butter in small saucepan. Pour into a small bowl and blend in powdered sugar, vanilla and Pre-Melted Cocoa Bake. Stir in enough hot water to make mixture smooth. Put glaze in a glass measuring cup and pour over cake roll evenly, letting it run down the sides.

Sour Cream Pound Cake

Judy Baker — Phoenix

1/2 lb. butter
3 cups sugar
6 eggs
3 cups flour

1 (8 oz.) carton sour cream
1/2 tsp. baking powder
1 tsp. vanilla

Cream butter and sugar. Add eggs and beat well. Add flour, sour cream, baking powder and vanilla. Bake in greased and floured tube pan. Bake at 300° for 1 1/4 hours, or until done.

This cake is a favorite of our family for strawberry short cake. It can also be a coffee cake if you put Coffee Cake Filling in the middle and a glaze on top.

Coffee Cake Filling

1/2 stick butter
1 tsp. cinnamon

brown sugar
walnuts

Combine butter and cinnamon and add brown sugar until mixture is of cornmeal consistency. Add walnuts.

Golden Angel Cake

Sharon Ann Kretschmar — Phoenix

8 large eggs
1 1/2 tsp. cream of tartar
1/4 tsp. salt
1 1/2 cups sugar (divided use)
1 tsp. vanilla, lemon or orange extract
1 cup + 2 Tbsp. all-purpose flour, sifted

Separate yolks from whites in large bowls. Sift flour with 1/2 cup sugar 3 times. Beat yolks till frothy then add 1/2 cup sugar and beat till thick and lemon colored. Beat whites till frothy, add salt, cream of tartar and beat till they stand in peaks. Then add 1/2 cup sugar and beat till glossy. Add extract. Fold yolks into whites. Then fold in flour 2 to 3 Tbsp. at a time. Turn into ungreased tube pan and bake at 300° for 40 minutes and an additional 15 minutes at 325°. Invert pan to cool.

Although time consuming to make, this cake is worth the effort. Using both whites and yokes of the egg produces a moister cake than most angels.

When I entered this cake in the Fair, it caused a small problem of just how to classify it. It is made as a traditional angel and looks like an angel, but because of the yokes it does not taste like an angel cake.

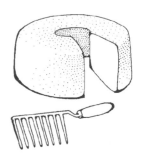

Orange Chiffon Cake

Robert Markey — Phoenix

2 1/4 cups cake flour
1 1/2 cups sugar
1 Tbsp. salt.
1 tsp. baking soda
1/2 cup oil
6 egg yolks
1/4 cup water
1/2 cup orange juice (fresh)
orange zest, finely chopped
1 Tbsp. vanilla.
1 cup egg whites

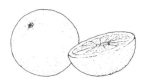

Sift together the flour, 3/4 cup of the sugar, baking powder and salt. In a separate bowl mix the oil, yolks, water, juice, zest and vanilla. Add the liquid mixture to the dry.

In a clean bowl beat the egg whites until foamy. Slowly beat in the remaining 3/4 cup of sugar. Continue beating until whites are stiff but not dry. Stir 1/3 of the whites into the batter to lighten it. Fold in the remaining whites. Pour the batter into an ungreased 10" tube pan. Bake at 325° for about one hour, until a toothpick comes out clean. Immediately invert the pan over the neck of a bottle. Allow the cake to "hang" upside down until completely cool. Remove the cake from the pan.

Orange Glaze

2/3 cup confectioners' sugar
2 Tbsp. orange juice
2 tsp. orange zest

Stir ingredients together in a small bowl. Drizzle over top of cooled cake.

Honey Spice Cake

Louise Matlock — Scottsdale

1 cup hot water
1 tsp. instant coffee powder
4 eggs, separated
3/4 cup sugar
1 cup honey
1/2 cup cooking oil

3 cups sifted flour
1/2 tsp. salt
2 tsp. baking powder
1 tsp. baking soda
1/2 tsp. ground cloves
1/2 tsp. allspice

Mix hot water with instant coffee; set aside. Separate eggs. Beat yolks with sugar until creamy; add cooking oil, then honey, beating after each addition until mixture is smooth and creamy. Combine flour, salt, baking powder, soda and spices. Add dry ingredients to honey-egg mixture alternately with coffee, mixing only until well blended. Do not over mix. Beat egg whites until stiff, but not dry. Fold into honey-egg batter.

Bake in greased and floured 12-cup Bundt pan at 325° for 50 minutes or until toothpick tests clean. Cool 10-15 minutes. Turn out on cake plate to complete cooling. Frost with ***Brown Butter Glaze.***

Brown Butter Glaze

1/2 cup butter
juice of 1/2 orange
2 cups sifted powdered sugar

In small saucepan melt butter until golden brown. Add orange juice. Cool. Add to powdered sugar and stir until smooth.

Feathery Fudge Cake

Joan Messerschmidt — Phoenix

2/3 cup butter
2 eggs
1 3/4 cup sugar
1 tsp. vanilla
2 1/2 squares baking chocolate
2 1/2 cups sifted cake flour
1/2 tsp. salt
1 1/4 tsp. baking soda
1 1/4 cups ice water

Cream together for 5 minutes butter, eggs, sugar, and vanilla.

Blend in 2 1/2 squares of melted baking chocolate. Sift together cake flour, salt and baking soda. Add sifted mixture to batter alternately with ice water. Bake in two greased 8" round cake pans at 350° for 30-35 minutes.

Ice Cream Frosting

Blend together: **1 cup milk, 6 Tbsp. flour.** Cook over low heat, stirring constantly until very thick. Chill.

Cream together: **1/2 cup butter, 1/2 cup shortening, 1 cup sugar, 1 tsp. vanilla.** Beat 4 minutes. Add chilled mixture and beat for 4 more minutes.

I have entered this recipe several times since I was in high school. It always wins a 2nd place ribbon and in 1993 it won a 1st place blue ribbon!

Sparky's Favorite Carrot Cake

Kathy Mills — Phoenix

2 cups sugar
1 1/3 cups vegetable oil
4 eggs
2 cups cake flour

2 tsp. baking soda
2 tsp. cinnamon
1 tsp. salt
3 cups grated carrots

Grease and flour 9 x 13 pan. Preheat oven to 350°. Mix together sugar, eggs and oil. Add flour, soda, cinnamon, salt, and carrots. Pour batter into prepared pan and bake for one hour. Cool cake at least one hour before icing.

Icing

8 oz. soft cream cheese
1 cup softened butter
1 cup chopped toasted almonds

1 box powdered sugar
2 tsp. vanilla

Mix all icing ingredients and whip until smooth. (Hint: I use my food processor for this.)

Pound Cake

Joyce Lopez — Phoenix

1 cup butter
3 cups sugar
3 cups flour
1 tsp. soda
6 eggs (separated)

1 (16 oz.) carton sour cream
2 tsp. lemon or vanilla flavoring

Grease and flour a 12-cup fluted tube pan. Beat egg whites until stiff; then set aside. Cream butter and sugar together, add egg yolks and beat well. Add flour, soda and sour cream alternately, starting with flour. Beat well after each addition. Fold in egg whites and pour into pan. Bake at 325° for 1 1/2 hours or until tester comes out clean. Cool in pan, turn out on cake plate and dust with powdered sugar.

Banana Sour Cream Cake

Louise Perkins — Glendale

1 cup granulated sugar
1/2 cup softened margarine
2 eggs
1 1/2 cups mashed ripe bananas
3/4 cup sour cream
1 tsp. vanilla
1 1/2 cups flour
1 1/2 tsp. baking powder
1 tsp. baking soda
1/2 tsp. cinnamon
1 cup quick oats
1 cup chopped walnuts

Cream the sugar and butter until smooth. Beat in mashed bananas, sour cream and vanilla. Stir together flour, baking powder, baking soda and cinnamon. Beat into the banana mixture. Stir in the oats and nuts. Pour into greased Bundt or tube pan.

Bake in 350° oven for 35-45 minutes (or until inserted toothpick comes out clean). Allow cake to cool in pan for about 15 minutes; then remove to cooling rack. Combine **1 cup powdered sugar** and **1 1/2 Tbsp. milk** and drizzle over the completely cooled cake.

German Sweet Chocolate Cake

Marie Thomas — Phoenix

1 pkg. (4 oz.) German sweet chocolate
1/2 cup boiling water
1 cup butter or margarine
2 cups sugar
4 egg yolks
1 tsp. vanilla
2 1/2 cups sifted cake flour
1 tsp. baking soda
1/2 tsp. salt
1 cup buttermilk
4 egg whites, stiffly beaten

Melt chocolate in boiling water. Cool. Cream butter and sugar until fluffy. Add yolks, one at a time, beating well after each. Blend in vanilla and chocolate. Sift flour with soda and salt; add alternately with buttermilk to chocolate mixture, beating after each addition until smooth. Fold in beaten whites. Pour into three 8" or 9" layer pans, lined on bottoms with paper. Bake at 350° for 30 to 40 minutes. Cool. Frost tops only.

Coconut Pecan Frosting

Combine **1 cup evaporated milk, 1 cup sugar, 3 slightly beaten egg yolks, 1/2 cup butter or margarine,** and **1 tsp. vanilla.** Cook and stir over medium heat until thickened (about 12 minutes). Add **1 1/3 cups coconut** and **1 cup chopped pecans.** Cool until thick enough to spread; beat occasionally. Makes 2 1/2 cups.

Our Special
Birthday Cake

Bebe J. Reed — Nogales

1 cup shortening
3 cups cake flour
1 Tbsp. baking powder
1 1/2 tsp. vanilla
1 cup milk
1/2 cup chopped cherries

2 cups sugar
4 eggs, separated
1/4 tsp. salt
1/2 tsp. almond flavoring
3/4 cup chocolate chips

Cream shortening and sugar until fluffy. Beat egg yolks; add and beat well. Stir in flavorings. Sift dry ingredients together and add alternately with milk. Beat well after each addition. Fold in chips and cherries. Beat egg whites until stiff but not dry. Fold into batter. Pour into three 9" greased and floured pans. Bake at 375° about 30 minutes.

This cake is good with butterscotch chips, mint chips and, if you can get them, the cherry, coconut and blueberry chips that are available in the mid-west. To make these for small children I use mini chips and cupcake pans.

Chocolate Buttercream Frosting

1 lb. of softened butter
2 lb. pkg. of powdered sugar
6 Tbsp. vanilla (or other flavoring)
3/4 cup cocoa

Add sugar to butter a little at a time. Beat well after each addition. When frosting becomes stiff, add flavoring, beat well. Add cocoa, beat well.

Add sugar alternately with milk. Be sure to end with milk. If too stiff to spread, add more milk 1 teaspoonful at a time until proper consistency.

This family favorite recipe was passed down to Bebe from her mother and grandmother.

Pecan-Streusel Coffee Cake

Beth Sternitzky — Apache Junction

1/2 cup butter
3/4 cup sugar
1 tsp. vanilla
2 eggs
1 cup sour cream

2 cups flour
1 tsp. baking powder
1/2 tsp. baking soda
1/4 tsp. salt

Melt butter and place in a mixing bowl. Cool. Add sugar, vanilla, eggs and sour cream. Whisk together and set aside. Sift the dry ingredients together and combine with butter mixture. Mix well and turn into a greased 9 x 9 pan. Put *Topping* on batter in pan.

Topping

1 cup cut up pecans
1/2 cup packed brown sugar
1/2 cup flour

3 Tbsp. butter,
    softened
2 tsp. vanilla

Mix ingredients together well with a fork and crumble on top of cake in the pan. Bake for 1 hour at 325° or until done (test with a toothpick). Cool on rack. Excellent served warm. May be frozen for future use.

Coconut-Carrot Cake

Terri Topliss — Peoria

1 3/4 cups all-purpose flour
2 tsp. cinnamon
2 cups sugar
4 large eggs
2 cups shredded carrots
1 cup flaked coconut

2 tsp. baking soda
1 tsp. salt
1 1/2 cups oil
2 tsp. vanilla extract
8 oz. crushed pineapple,
   drained

1/2 cup golden raisins   1 cup chopped pecans   Preheat oven to 350°. Grease and flour three (8") square cake pans. Combine flour, baking soda, cinnamon and salt. In large bowl of electric mixer, at high speed, beat sugar, oil, eggs and vanilla until blended. Stir in carrots, pineapple, coconut, chopped pecans and raisins. Pour batter into cake pans. Bake 30 minutes. Cool cakes completely, on wire racks. Place one cake layer on serving platter, spread 1/2 cup *Cream Cheese Frosting* over top of cake. Repeat for other two layers. Spread a thin layer of frosting on sides of cake. Fill pastry bag with remaining frosting. Decorate sides of cake with tip #21 making solid vertical lines, from top to bottom. Arrange pecan halves around top edge of cake. Sprinkle remaining pecan halves on the top of the cake.

Cream Cheese Frosting

20 oz. cream cheese
1/2 cup butter
1 tsp. vanilla
3/4 cup confectioners' sugar
1/4 tsp. cinnamon

Beat cream cheese, butter and vanilla with electric mixer until fluffy. Gradually beat in sugar and cinnamon at medium speed until blended.

Chocolate Walnut Rum Cake

Patricia Urton — Scottsdale

1 3/4 cups cake flour
1 tsp. soda
3/4 tsp. baking powder
3/4 tsp. salt
1/2 cup + 1 Tbsp. Butter
 Flavor Crisco®
1 1/2 cups sugar

3 oz. melted bittersweet
 chocolate
1 tsp. vanilla
2 large eggs
1 cup milk (room
 temperature)

Sift together first four ingredients. Beat together Crisco and sugar on medium speed for about 2 minutes. At low speed mix chocolate, vanilla, and eggs; add to Crisco and sugar mixture. Mix in dry ingredients alternately with milk, beginning and ending with dry ingredients.

Grease and flour four 8-inch or three 9-inch pans. Pour batter equally into pans; bake at 350° for 35 to 40 minutes or until tester comes out clean. Turn out onto racks to cool, wrap and store overnight.

Syrup

Combine **1/2 cup water** and **1/4 cup sugar** in a small saucepan. Bring to a boil over medium heat and boil until sugar dissolves. Remove from heat and add **1/4 cup dark rum.** Store at room temperature.

Filling

6 Tbsp. unsalted butter
1 1/4 cups heavy
 whipping cream

12 oz. semisweet chocolate
1 Tbsp. vanilla
1/2 cup ground walnuts

In heavy sauce pan melt butter in whipping cream. Remove from heat and add chocolate and mix till smooth. Refrigerate until just cool and still soft (about 40 minutes). Stir occasionally. Add vanilla and ground walnuts. Mix well and let stand at room temperature.

(Continued on next page)

(*Chocolate Walnut Rum Cake* continued from previous page)

Glaze

1 cup unsalted butter
2 cups heavy whipping cream
4 Tbsp. light corn syrup
16 oz. bittersweet chocolate
walnut halves

In a heavy saucepan melt butter in whipping cream and corn syrup. Remove from heat and add chocolate and stir until smooth. Dip walnut halves in mixture and place on lightly buttered wax paper. Place in refrigerator until chocolate is firm. Let remaining glaze cool until luke warm (about 30 minutes), stirring occasionally.

Place a layer of cake on cake plate and drizzle with syrup. Add second layer and cover with filling. Continue layering, alternating syrup and filling until all layers are done. Spread remaining glaze over sides of cake and decorate with chocolate dipped walnuts.

Yummy Banana Nut Cake

Mary Panis — Phoenix

1 1/2 cups sugar
1/2 cup shortening
1/4 tsp. salt
1 tsp. vanilla
2 beaten eggs

1 cup mashed bananas
1/2 cup buttermilk
2 cups flour
1 tsp. baking soda
3/4 cup chopped nuts

Cream sugar and shortening. Add salt, vanilla and eggs. Beat well. Add bananas and buttermilk alternately. Sift flour and baking soda; mix with rest. Add chopped nuts and pour into greased and lightly floured 9 x 13 pan or Bundt pan. Bake 30 to 35 minutes in 350° oven.

Frost with favorite vanilla frosting or combine **1/2 cup powdered sugar, 1/2 tsp. vanilla** and **2 to 3 tsp. milk** and drizzle over cooled cake. Sprinkle with nuts if desired.

Cheesecake

Pam Wilson — Chandler

1 1/2 lbs. cream cheese
1 pint sour cream
3/4 cup sugar
6 eggs, separated
2 tsp. flour
1 tsp. vanilla
1 box (3 cups crushed) zwieback
  or graham crackers
1/4 lb. melted butter

Crush crackers till fine and add melted butter. Press this mixture onto the bottom and sides of 10-inch springform pan. Refrigerate.

Separate eggs; beat whites until stiff. Mash cream cheese and sour cream together until they make a smooth paste. Add sugar, flour, salt, yolks and vanilla. Blend well. Fold in whites (don't worry about lumps). Put in cake pan. On the lowest rack of oven place a baking pan full of water. Place cake pan on rack right above water. Bake 55 to 60 minutes in 350° oven. Do not open oven door till done. Remove pan of water but leave cake in oven for another hour with the oven door open. Refrigerate.

Pam is an LPN at Thomas Davis Medical Center in Tempe. She loves cooking, reading and traveling. She's also on a hot air balloon chase crew.

COOKIE RECIPES

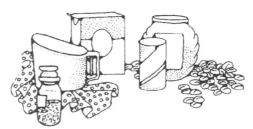

Orange Citrus Cookies

Jan Herrmann-Beach — Mesa

1/2 cup butter
1 cup sugar
1 egg
1/2 cup sour milk or
　substitute 1/2 Tbsp.
　lemon juice & 1/2 cup milk

3 to 3 1/2 cups flour
1/2 tsp. baking soda
1 tsp. baking powder
1 tsp. orange extract
2 tsp. grated orange peel
1/3 cup orange juice

Cream the butter and sugar. Add the egg, slightly beaten. Combine flour, baking soda and baking powder, and add to the sugar mixture. Add orange extract, orange peel and orange juice and mix well. Drop by spoonful on lightly sprayed cookie sheet. Bake at 375° for 10-12 minutes.

When cooled, frost with **Orange Icing**. Makes 1 to 2 dozen 2 to 3 inch cookies.

Orange Icing

3 Tbsp. softened butter
1/2 to 1 cup powdered sugar
red food coloring
yellow food coloring

Stir the butter and sugar together. Mix to desired consistency and add a drop each of red and yellow food coloring. Frost cooled cookies.

I remember the cookies my grandmother used to make when I was a child; how they would melt in my mouth and how wonderful they smelled. But my grandmother died long before I learned how to bake. After spending some 35 years looking for the perfect recipe, I decided to create my own, and here is the result. Grandma would be proud, especially since my cookies won a blue ribbon.

Ginger Snaps

Karen A. Buchanan — Mesa

2/3 cup Wesson® Oil
1 cup sugar
1 egg
1/4 cup unsulphured molasses
2 cups flour
1/4 cup sugar for dipping

2 tsp. baking soda
1/2 tsp. ground cloves
1/2 tsp. salt
1 tsp. cinnamon
1 tsp. ginger

Blend oil and sugar thoroughly. Add eggs; beat well. Stir in molasses. Sift dry ingredients; add to mix. Drop by teaspoonfuls into sugar and roll into balls. Place on ungreased cookie sheet 3 inches apart. Bake at 350° for 7 1/2 to 8 minutes (cookies will flatten and crinkle).

Date Filled Cookies

Carol Fortier — Phoenix

1 cup shortening
2 cups brown sugar
2 eggs
1/2 cup water or milk
1 tsp. vanilla

3 1/2 cups flour
1 tsp. salt
1 tsp. soda
1/4 tsp. cinnamon
1/8 tsp. ginger

Mix shortening, sugar and eggs together. Stir in water (or milk) and vanilla. Sift together flour, salt, soda, cinnamon and ginger; add to shortening mixture. Drop by the teaspoonful onto ungreased cookie sheet. Place a little of the *Filling* on top of each and cover with just a bit more cookie batter. Bake at 400° until golden brown.

Filling

2 cups dates (cut)   3/4 cup sugar   3/4 cup water

In a saucepan, combine ingredients and heat. Add to top of cookies before baking.

Rich's Ginger Snaps

Norma Eakin — Chandler

1/2 cup margarine	1/4 tsp. salt
1/4 cup shortening	2 tsp. soda
1/4 cup molasses	1/2 tsp. cloves
1 egg	1/2 tsp ginger
1/2 cup brown sugar	1 tsp. cinnamon
2 cups flour	1/2 cup sugar

Melt margarine and shortening together in saucepan. Remove from heat and add molasses. Slowly stir in beaten egg and brown sugar. Combine flour, salt, soda and spices. Stir in molasses mixture. Chill several hours or overnight. Roll dough in small balls and coat with sugar. Place on baking sheet, but do not flatten. Bake at 375° for 8 to 10 minutes or until slightly brown around the edges. Cookies will flatten while baking. Allow to cool on baking sheet about 2 minutes before removing to let harden.

Store in tightly covered container and hide it if you want to keep them.

Peanut Butter Cookies

Patti Contreras — Stanfield

1 1/4 cups flour	1/2 cup (packed) brown sugar
3/4 tsp. baking soda	
1/4 tsp. salt	1/2 cup sugar
1/2 cup butter	1 egg
3/4 cup peanut butter	1/2 tsp. vanilla

Stir together flour, soda and salt. Beat butter, add peanut butter and sugars, add egg and vanilla. Add dry ingredients to beaten mixture and roll into 1-inch balls. Roll in granulated sugar. Crisscross with fork. Bake on ungreased cookie sheet at 375° for 10 minutes.

Fudgy Caramel Wedges

Jody Hall — Phoenix

2 oz. (2 squares) semisweet chocolate, chopped
1 oz. (1 square) unsweetened chocolate, chopped
1/2 cup margarine or butter
3/4 cup flour
3/4 cup sugar
2 eggs
1 Tbsp. vanilla
1/2 cup coarsely chopped pecans

Heat oven to 325°. Line 9" round cake pan with foil; grease. In medium saucepan over low heat, melt semisweet chocolate, unsweetened chocolate and margarine, stirring constantly. Cool slightly. Lightly spoon flour into measuring cup; level off. Combine flour, sugar, vanilla, eggs and chocolate mixture; blend well. Pour into prepared pan. Sprinkle nuts over batter. Bake at 325° for 20 to 30 minutes or until set.

Topping

10 vanilla caramels
2 Tbsp. milk
1/2 oz. (1/2 square) unsweetened chocolate, chopped
2 tsp. margarine or butter
1 tsp. light corn syrup

In small saucepan over low heat, melt caramels and milk, stirring frequently until smooth. Drizzle over bars. In same saucepan over low heat, melt unsweetened chocolate, margarine and corn syrup. Drizzle over bars. Cool completely; cut into wedges. 12 to 16 servings.

Having raised 6 children and now with the addition of 8 grandchildren, 5 sons and daughters-in-law, I am required to have recipes and cookies for all occasions.

Honey Cookies

Chris Heath — Phoenix

3 cups all-purpose flour
1 tsp. baking soda
1/2 tsp. salt
2 tsp. ground cinnamon
1/2 tsp. ground cloves
1 tsp. ground allspice
1 tsp. grated nutmeg
1/2 tsp. ground ginger
4 oz. candied orange peel (finely ground or minced)
1 cup finely ground walnuts (lightly toasted
    and cooled)
1 cup fragrant honey
3/4 cup brown sugar
1 egg
1 Tbsp. fresh lemon juice
1 Tbsp. fresh orange juice (can substitute rum or
    brandy)
2 tsp. finely grated lemon zest
1 tsp. finely grated orange zest

Sift flour, soda, salt, and spices together. Lightly mix the candied peel and walnuts together. Warm the honey in a small pan; remove from heat. In a large bowl, with an electric mixer at medium speed, cream brown sugar and egg until smooth and fluffy; add lemon and orange juices, honey and lemon and orange zests. Beat well. Add flour mixture one cup at a time. Finally add candied peel and nuts. Mix well. You may have to finish the dough by hand. Cover and refrigerate overnight.

Preheat oven to 375°. On a lightly floured surface (pastry cloth is best) roll out dough (half at a time) to slightly thicker than 1/4". Using a sharp 2" cookie cutter, cut out cookies as close together as possible. (Dough can be rolled in a square and cut with a knife to prevent re-rolling toughness of excess dough.) Grease and flour cookie sheets or line them with parchment.

(Continued on next page)

(*Honey Cookies* continued)

Place cookies on sheets 2 to 3 inches apart; bake them for 12 to 14 minutes until slightly brown but still soft. Remove to racks to cool. Store tightly covered in a cool dry place for at least 3 weeks to ripen. If cookies are dry, place apple slice in container for a few days. Yields 2-3 dozen.

Glaze: The day before serving: Glaze cooled cookies with **honey** brought to a boil and cooled to just warm. While honey is still wet, decorate with cherry halves and sliced almonds. Allow cookies to air dry overnight.

Cowpies
(Beef Cookies)
Susan L. Krevitsky Law — Phoenix

3/4 cup shortening	1 tsp. salt
1 cup (packed) brown sugar	1 tsp. cinnamon
1/2 cup sugar	2 tsp. soda
1 egg	1/2 tsp. cloves
1/4 cup water	1 cup raisins
1 tsp. vanilla	1 cup chopped nuts
1 cup flour	1 cup cooked ground
3 cups quick cooking oats	beef

Heat oven to 350°. Mix shortening, sugars, egg, water and vanilla. Stir in everything else. Drop by rounded spoonfuls onto ungreased cookie sheet. Bake 12-15 mins. Store in tightly covered container. Makes 5 dozen.

I have been entering the Arizona State Fair since I was nine years old (now 23 years). The very first thing I ever entered were Ginger Snaps and I won a blue ribbon. I always enter Ginger Snaps in the Fair in tribute to my humble beginnings. It's a given that I'm going to enter the Fair every year. It's a family tradition.

I inherited my love of baking from my mom, Thelma, and my dad, Chuck, both of whom are Arizona State Fair winners, as is my sister, Robin. We must have flour in our blood!

Peanut Popcorn Crisp

Maralee Johnson — Laveen

Pop **1/2 pound popcorn** and put in a large kettle in moderate 300° oven.

1 1/2 cups white sugar
1 cup brown sugar
5/8 cup light corn syrup
3/4 cup water

Combine sugars, syrup and water in a heavy saucepan. Bring to a boil. Wash sides down and then add: **1 tsp. salt,** cook to 270°, add **1 1/2 cups raw Spanish peanuts,** cook to 300° and add **1/2 cube (2 oz.) butter or margarine.** When butter is well mixed in, take pan off of burner and add **1 tsp. soda** mixed with **1 tsp. vanilla.** Stir well.

Immediately take the corn out of the oven. Scrape all of the syrup into the corn and mix the whole thing together until the corn is well coated. Pour out onto a cold slab (does not need to be oiled) and spread thin while still hot.

Remember — it takes 212° of heat to cause water to boil at sea level. Since no water leaves the batch until it does boil, the start of the cooking is really the boiling point. As the consistency of the batch of candy depends on the number of degrees the batch cooks above the boiling point, we must adjust our formulas to the altitude at which we live.

Put your candy thermometer in cold water, bring the water to a rolling boil and note the degree of heat registered. Subtract it from 212 degrees. Then subtract this difference from the degree of cooking given in this recipe.

Sugar Cookies

Carol Hardin — Phoenix

2 cups sugar
1 stick margarine
2 tsp. soda
1 tsp. vanilla

1/2 cup shortening
3 eggs
4 1/2 cups flour

Cream together sugar, shortening and margarine. Mix in remaining ingredients. Mix well; may be necessary to knead dough to get all the flour mixed in.

Chill, roll out, and cut in desired shapes. Bake on greased cookie sheet in 350° oven for 12 minutes. Decorate as desired.

I am a grandmother and have used this recipe for many years to make cookies for my children and now my grandchildren.

Peanut Butter Swirls

Jetaun Hollingsworth — Tempe

1/2 cup shortening
1 cup sugar
1/2 cup chunky peanut butter
1 egg
2 Tbsp. milk

1 1/2 cups sifted flour
1/2 tsp. salt
1/2 tsp. baking soda
1 (6 oz.) pkg. semisweet
  chocolate chips

Cream shortening and sugar until light. Beat in peanut butter, egg and milk. Sift together flour, salt, and baking soda; stir into creamed mixture. Place dough on lightly floured waxed paper. Roll in 15 x 8 x 1/4 inch rectangles. Melt chocolate over hot water. Cool slightly and spread over dough. Roll like jelly roll, lifting wax paper slightly with each turn Chill 1/2 hour. Slice cookies 1/4 inch thick. Place on ungreased baking sheet. Bake at 375° 6-10 minutes. Makes 4 dozen.

Frosted
Orange Date Bars

Betty C. Ketchum — Mesa

3/4 cup sugar
1/2 cup butter or margarine
1/2 cup water
1 (8 oz.) pkg. chopped dates
1 1/4 cups all-purpose flour
1 cup chopped pecans

3/4 cup milk
1/4 cup orange juice
2 eggs
3/4 tsp. baking soda
1/2 tsp. salt
1 Tbsp. grated orange
  peel

Heat oven to 350°. In 3-quart saucepan combine sugar, butter, water and dates. Cook over low heat, stirring constantly until dates are softened. Remove from heat. By hand, stir in remaining bar ingredients until well mixed. Spread into greased 15 x 10 x 1 jelly roll pan. Bake for 15-20 minutes or until toothpick comes out clean. Cool completely.

Frosting

3 cups powdered sugar
1/3 cup butter or margarine (softened)
3 oz. cream cheese (softened)
1 Tbsp. grated orange peel
2 to 3 Tbsp. orange juice

In a small mixer bowl combine all ingredients and beat at medium speed, scraping bowl often. Spread over cooled bars and cut into bars.

Banana Bars

Penney Kopp — Phoenix

1 1/2 cups sugar
1/2 cup soft margarine
1 cup sour cream
2 eggs
1 1/2 cups mashed bananas

2 tsp. vanilla
2 cups flour
1 tsp. soda
3/4 tsp. salt
1/2 cup chopped nuts

Heat oven to 375°. Grease and flour jelly roll pan. Mix sugar, margarine, sour cream and eggs for 1 minute. Beat in bananas and vanilla. Beat in flour, soda and salt for 1 minute. Stir in nuts. Bake 20-25 minutes. Cool and frost with **Butter Frosting**.

Butter Frosting

Heat **1/4 cup margarine** over medium heat until lightly brown. Remove from heat and mix in **2 cups powdered sugar**. Beat in **1 tsp. vanilla** and **3 Tbsp. of milk** until smooth.

San Dabs

(Mexican Wedding Cookies)

Elnora Westfall — Phoenix

1 cup butter
1/2 cup powdered sugar
1 egg white (unbeaten)
2 cups all-purpose flour

1/4 tsp. salt
1 tsp. vanilla
1/2 cup finely
   chopped nuts

Cream butter and sugar and blend in egg white. Add the flour, salt and vanilla and blend well. Add the nuts and mix until the dough holds together. Shape into one inch (1") balls and place on an ungreased cookie sheet one inch (1") apart. Flatten slightly and bake 20 minutes at 250° or just until set, but not brown. Roll in powdered sugar while warm and again when cool.

*Word of advice from Elnora. I learned the hard way!
Never use "light" margarines. They contain much too
much water and cookies spread out too thin.*

Big Nose Katie's Chocolate Chip Cookies

Joyce Lopez — Phoenix

2 1/4 cups all-purpose flour
1 tsp. baking soda
1 tsp. salt
1 cup Parkay® soft margarine
3/4 cup sugar
3/4 cup (packed) brown sugar
1 tsp. vanilla
2 eggs
1 (12 oz.) pkg. Nestlé® Semi-Sweet Chocolate Morsels
1 cup chopped black walnuts
1/3 cup Frangelica® liqueur

Preheat oven to 350°. In a small bowl, combine flour, baking soda, and salt. Set aside. In large bowl combine butter, sugar, brown sugar and vanilla extract and beat until creamy. Beat in eggs. Gradually add flour mixture and mix well. Stir in Nestle semisweet chips, nuts and Frangelica. Drop by spoonfuls onto ungreased cookie sheets. Bake at 375° for 8 to 10 minutes.

Big Nose Katie, our bloodhound, always supervises the preparation and baking of these cookies. She sits by the stove and tells us when to remove them from the oven via her keen nose and watchful eye on the oven door. Hope you enjoy.

Hermits

Violet McClure — Phoenix

1 cup shortening
2 cups brown sugar (packed)
2 eggs
1/2 cup cold coffee
3 1/2 cups Gold Medal® Flour
1 tsp. soda

1 tsp. salt
1 tsp. nutmeg
1 tsp. cinnamon
2 1/2 cups raisins
1 1/4 cups broken nuts

Mix shortening, sugar and eggs thoroughly. Stir in coffee. Measure flour by dipping method or by sifting. Stir dry ingredients together; blend into shortening mixture. Mix in raisins and nuts. Chill dough at least 1 hour.

Heat oven to 400°. Drop rounded teaspoonfuls of dough about 2" apart on lightly greased baking sheet. Bake 8 to 10 minutes. Makes 7 to 8 doz., 2 1/2 " cookies.

Butterscotch Chewy Bars

Mary Jane McHenry — Phoenix

1 1/2 cups flour
3/4 cup granulated sugar
1/4 cup brown sugar
1 3/4 tsp. baking powder
1/4 tsp. baking soda
1/4 tsp. salt
1 cup toffee chips

1/4 cup shortening
1 egg
1/4 cup water
1 Tbsp. corn syrup
1/3 cup chocolate chips
1/2 cup chopped nuts

Combine wet and dry ingredients, except for toffee chips. Drop by teaspoonful on baking sheets lined with baking paper. (Or, sheets may be lightly greased.) Bake at 350° about 7 minutes. Sprinkle toffee chips on top immediately and return to the oven for 1 to 2 minutes. Makes about 2 dozen cookies.

Soft Molasses Cookies

Laurine McGhee — Phoenix

1/2 cup butter, softened
1/2 cup vegetable shortening (not margarine)
1 1/2 cups sugar
1/2 cup molasses
2 eggs, lightly beaten
4 cups all-purpose flour
1/2 tsp. salt
2 1/4 tsp. baking soda
2 1/4 tsp. ground ginger
1 1/2 tsp. ground cloves
1 1/2 tsp. ground cinnamon
additional sugar

In a large mixing bowl, cream together butter, shortening and sugar until light colored and fluffy. Beat in molasses and eggs; set aside. In another large bowl, combine flour (no need to sift), salt, baking soda, ginger, cloves and cinnamon. Blend thoroughly with wire whisk. Gradually mix flour mixture into creamed ingredients until dough is blended and smooth. Roll dough into 1 1/2 inch balls. Dip tops in sugar and place 2 1/2 inches apart on greased cookie sheets. Bake in 350° oven for 11 minutes. Do not overbake. Cool on wire rack. Store in tightly covered container to maintain softness. Yields about 3 dozen cookies.

To keep them soft and chewy, store in container with a slice of raw apple. These cookies freeze beautifully, too.

I have always liked to cook and bake. I am constantly trying new recipes. This recipe has been a favorite with my children, grandchildren and great-grandchildren.

Peanut Butter Cookies

Marla Neveils — Phoenix

1 cup shortening
1/2 tsp. salt
1 cup peanut butter
1 cup sugar
1 cup (packed) brown sugar

2 eggs well-beaten
1 Tbsp. milk
2 cups flour
1/2 tsp. baking soda

Combine shortening, salt and peanut butter. Mix well. Gradually add sugar and brown sugar. Cream thoroughly. Add eggs and milk; mix well. Sift together the flour and soda. Blend with creamed mixture. Drop the dough by teaspoonfuls on greased cookie sheet, or form into balls and press with a fork. Bake at 350° approximately 8 minutes.

My mother came across this recipe when she was a little girl and passed it on to me. It has remained a family favorite.

Date 'n Nut Bars

Sylvia Noll — Tempe

2 eggs
1/2 cup granulated sugar
1/2 tsp. vanilla
1/2 cup flour
1/2 tsp. baking powder

1/2 tsp. salt
2 cups finely chopped
  pitted dates
1 cup chopped walnuts

Preheat oven 325° Grease a 9 x 13 x 2 pan. Beat eggs in a large bowl until foamy. Add sugar and vanilla to the beaten eggs. Sift flour, baking powder, and salt together. Stir dry ingredients into the egg mixture. Mix in the dates and nuts. Spread in the prepared pan. Bake in a moderate oven at 325° for 25 to 30 minutes or until top has a dull crust. Cool and cut into bars. Dust with powdered sugar before serving.

Raisin Date Cookies

Opha Probasco — Tucson

1 cup margarine
3/4 cup granulated sugar
3/4 cup brown sugar
2 eggs
zest from 1 orange
zest from 1 lemon
2 1/2 cups all-purpose flour
1 tsp. baking soda

1 tsp. ground cinnamon
1/4 tsp. nutmeg
1/8 tsp. cloves
1 pkg. (9 oz.) raisins
1 cup chopped dates
1 cup chopped walnuts
   or pecans

Beat margarine and sugars until fluffy. Add eggs and mix thoroughly. Add orange and lemon zest. Combine flour, baking soda, cinnamon, nutmeg and cloves. Stir into margarine mixture until blended. Add raisins, dates and nuts. Drop by tablespoonfuls onto ungreased cookie sheet. Bake in 375° oven 10 to 13 minutes or to a light golden brown. Cool on a wire rack.

Opha Probasco has been entering his baked goods in the Pima County Fair since 1993. Winning many 1st place ribbons and best in the class, as well as the C&H® Sugar and Clabber Girl® Baking Powder awards. He decided to try the Arizona State Fair in 1994 and won a blue ribbon for this recipe.

Chocolate Chip Cookies

Brenda L. Strom — Gilbert

Preheat oven to 375°.

1 cup margarine
1 cup butter (made in Arizona preferred)
3/4 cup sugar
3/4 cup (packed) brown sugar
2 tsp. vanilla extract
2 eggs (from Arizona preferred)

Beat the margarine, butter, sugars and vanilla extract together until fluffy. (I prefer to use an electric mixer.) Add eggs, one at a time and beat until well mixed.

1 1/4 cups white flour
1 tsp. baking soda
1 tsp. salt

Gradually add the flour, baking soda and salt to the above mixture until well blended.

18 ounces semisweet chocolate chips (I used the
**   gourmet store brand!)**
1 cup chopped walnuts

Fold chocolate chips and walnuts with previous mixture to make final cookie dough.

Scoop by the tablespoonful onto ungreased professional baking sheet. Bake at 375° for 8-9 minutes for chewy cookies and 10 minutes or longer for crunchy cookies. (I prefer the chewy cookies).

Venetians
(Petit Fours)

Mary L. Thibideau — Tempe

1 can (8 oz.) Solo® Almond Paste (not marzipan)
1 1/2 cups butter, softened
1 cup sugar
4 eggs, separated
1 1/2 tsp. almond extract
2 cups sifted all-purpose flour
1/4 tsp. salt
10 drops green food coloring
8 drops red food coloring
1 jar (12 oz.) apricot preserves
6 squares (1 oz. each) semisweet chocolate (6 oz.
   semisweet chips can be substituted)

Prepare three 13 x 9 x 2 inch baking pans by greasing pans and lining them with waxed paper. Then grease paper. Set aside.

Break up almond paste in large bowl with a fork. Add butter, sugar, egg yolks and almond extract. Beat with electric mixer until light and fluffy, about 5 minutes. Beat in flour and salt. Beat egg whites in medium-sized bowl with electric mixer until stiff peaks form. Fold into almond mixture with wooden spoon, using a turning motion.

Remove 1 1/2 cups batter; spread evenly into one of the prepared pans. Remove another 1 1/2 cups batter to a small bowl; tint with green food coloring. Spread evenly into second prepared pan. Add red food coloring to remaining 1 1/2 cups batter and spread into third prepared pan. Bake in preheated moderate 350° oven for 15 minutes or until edges are lightly golden. (Note: Cake layers will be 1/4" thick.) Immediately remove cakes from pans onto large wire racks. Remove wax paper gently if it sticks to cake and cool thoroughly.

(Continued on next page)

*(**Venetians** continued)*

Place green layer on upturned jelly-roll pan covered with waxed paper. Heat apricot preserves in small saucepan; strain, if desired. Spread half the warm preserves over green layer to edges. Place yellow layer on top. Spread with remaining preserves. Place pink layer, top-side up, on yellow layer. Cover with plastic wrap. Weigh down with large wooden cutting board or heavy flat tray. Refrigerate overnight. Melt chocolate in top of double boiler over hot water. Spread half of chocolate on one side of cake layer and let set (can refrigerate for faster setting). Turn cake over and spread remaining chocolate on second side and let set until firm. Trim cake edges even. Cut cake crosswise into 1" wide strips and into 1" pieces. Decorate with decorator rose buds, if desired.

I have enjoyed baking for many years and have a collection of wonderful recipes that have become both my family and friends/co-workers favorites. I was first introduced to these wonderful Petit Fours by an Italian friend who brought them to a Christmas Eve gathering at the home of a mutual friend. She was gracious enough to share her recipe with me. I have been making them ever since, especially as gifts for special friends at Christmas.

Fruit & Nut
Angel Drops

Paula Yeary — Glendale

1 cup butter, softened (no substitutions)
3/4 cup (packed) brown sugar
1 egg
1/2 tsp. vanilla extract
1 1/2 cups (rounded) all-purpose flour
1/2 tsp. salt
1/2 tsp. baking soda
4 oz. red candied cherries, halved
4 oz. candied pineapple, diced
1 cup dates, finely chopped
1/2 cup broken walnuts
1/2 cup broken pecans
1/2 cup whole macadamia nuts

In a mixing bowl cream butter, sugar, egg and vanilla. Sift together flour, salt and soda. Add to creamed mixture. Stir in fruits and nuts. Drop by teaspoonfuls onto greased cookie sheets. Bake at 325° for 15 minutes. Store in an air tight container.

Yields: 3 1/2 dozen.

Note: These cookies have a rich moist buttery flavor. They look pretty and tempting.

CANDY RECIPES

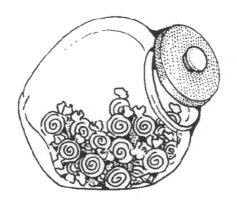

Easy Peanut Butter Fudge

Janet Rachfal — Glendale

3/4 cup (1 1/2 sticks) butter
1 jar (7 oz.) Kraft®
   Marshmallow Creme
2 1/4 cups sugar

1 tsp. pure vanilla
2/3 cup evaporated milk
1 cup Peter Pan® Extra
   Crunchy Peanut Butter

Mix butter, sugar and milk in heavy 3-quart saucepan. Bring to full boil, stirring constantly. Boil 5 minutes over medium heat, stirring constantly to prevent scorching. Remove from heat. Stir in peanut butter until melted and smooth. Add remaining ingredients; mix well.

Pour into 9" square baking pan lined with heavy duty foil. Cool to room temperature. Remove from pan and cut into squares.

Yields: approximately 2 1/2 lbs.

Peanut Butter Bon Bons

Joyce R. Waage — Glendale

1/2 cup margarine, melted
2 cups powdered sugar
2 cups Rice Krispies®

2 cups crunchy peanut
   butter

Combine all ingredients and mix well. Form into walnut size balls. Refrigerate 30 minutes or overnight.

Frosting

1 stick Parowax®   1 (12 oz.) bag of chocolate chips

Chop wax into small pieces. Put chips and wax into double boiler and melt, stirring continuously until all pieces are melted and blended well. Dip peanut butter balls in frosting and refrigerate. Makes 5 dozen.

Creamy Caramels

Pam Wilson — Chandler

1 1/2 cups half and half
1 1/2 cups whipping cream
2 tsp. vanilla
2 cups sugar

1 cup chopped toasted
   walnuts
1/4 tsp. salt
1 1/3 cups light corn syrup

Butter 9-inch square pan. Combine half and half and cream in 4 cup measure. Mix sugar, salt, corn syrup and 1 cup of the combined creams in heavy 3 or 4 quart saucepan. Cook over medium high heat, stirring constantly until syrup reaches 234° on candy thermometer (soft ball stage).

Add 1 more cup of cream and stir until mixture reaches 234°. Add remaining cream and stir until mixture reaches 250° (hard ball stage); this could take up to one hour. Remove from heat and stir in vanilla and nuts. Pour into pan and refrigerate until just firm but not hard. Cut in pieces about 1 inch square and wrap in cellophane, plastic wrap or waxed paper.

Molded Chocolate Shell

Virginia Burke — Phoenix

16 oz. semisweet or bittersweet chocolate
8 tsp. peanut or walnut oil
large flat shell and smaller shells

Melt chocolate and oil over hot water. Mix well.

Wrap a large flat shell with saran wrap. Coat the top of shell with melted chocolate, let set, and repeat. I use about four coats. When hard, carefully remove from the shell and keep cold. Peel off saran wrap.

Use candy mixture for molded small shell to put inside. I mixed colors for shells. I used chocolate, pink and white.

Peanut Brittle

Rosemary Lytle — Phoenix

3 cups granulated sugar
1 2/3 cups white Karo® syrup
1 1/3 cups water

Boil these three ingredients together till you can't stir down. Put lid on for 2 minutes and 50 seconds (over low heat). Then boil till it reaches 275° (over medium heat). Grease a marble slab or cookie sheet. Add **1/4 tsp. salt** and **1 stick of butter or margarine** to the sugar mixture. Add **1 lb. of unroasted Spanish peanuts** and stir until it reaches 300° (watch closely as it will burn). Add **1 tsp. vanilla** and a **heaping tsp. of baking soda.** Pour onto slab and let cool. Break into pieces. You may stretch the peanut brittle if you like, immediately after pouring on slab.

Divinity

Mary Komadina — Phoenix

3 cups sugar
3/4 cup light corn syrup
3/4 cup water
2 egg whites
1 tsp. vanilla
1 cup chopped nuts

Grease 9" square pan. Mix sugar, corn syrup and water in a saucepan and cook to boiling point, stirring constantly. Reduce heat and continue cooking, stirring occasionally until a few drops tested in cold water form a hard ball (250° on candy thermometer). Meanwhile beat egg whites until fluffy. Pour syrup into egg white mixture in thin, thin stream, beating constantly until candy holds peaks. Stir in vanilla and nuts. Quickly pour into pan. Dip knife in hot water during cutting.

Hard Molded Candy

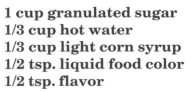

Betty C. Ketchum — Mesa

1 cup granulated sugar
1/3 cup hot water
1/3 cup light corn syrup
1/2 tsp. liquid food color
1/2 tsp. flavor

lollipop molds and sticks
candy thermometer
wooden spoon
vegetable oil

Combine sugar, hot water and corn syrup in a heavy 1 to 2 quart saucepan. Place on high heat. Stir with wooden spoon until sugar is dissolved. Continue cooking without stirring till temperature on candy thermometer reaches 300°. Remove from heat. Let stand until bubbles disappear. Add flavors and colors of choice. Stir to blend. Pour mixture into molds lightly brushed or sprayed with vegetable oil. Unmold.

Potato Candy

Chris Eaton — Phoenix

1/3 or 1/2 baked potato
1 box (16 oz.) confectioners' sugar
creamy or crunchy peanut butter

Peel the baked potato and mash. Gradually add the sugar to the mashed potato; it will eventually absorb the whole box.

Roll out the dough with a rolling pin. Spread with the peanut butter. Roll into a log. Chill for one hour. Slice the log into pieces of candy.

You will notice that the ingredients for this recipe are not very precise. That is because this recipe came from my paternal grandmother, Ada C. Zehrbach. She raised her family through the "Great Depression" and learned to make do with very little. Grandma always made this for us for Christmas, and we have continued with this tradition. Grandma passed away in the summer of 1994, at the age of 80. She would have been delighted to see her recipe shared with the readers of this cookbook.

Quick Penuche

Candace Rowland — Phoenix

2 cups whipping cream
1 Tbsp. light corn syrup
2 cups granulated sugar
1 cup firmly packed brown sugar
3 Tbsp. butter
1/2 cup (2 to 3 oz.) white
    compound coating
1 1/2 cups pecans, toasted

Line an 8-inch square baking pan with plastic wrap; set aside. In a heavy 4-quart saucepan, combine cream, corn syrup and sugars. Place over medium heat and stir with a wooden spoon until mixture comes to a boil. If sugar crystals are present, wash down sides of the pan with a wet pastry brush.

Clip on thermometer. Cook, stirring occasionally, to 236° (115°C) or soft-ball stage. Remove from heat. Without stirring, add butter. Let stand until thermometer cools to 210° (100°C). Without stirring, add compound coating. Let stand one minute. Remove thermometer. Add nuts and stir with a wooden spoon until coating is melted and butter is incorporated. Candy should be thick and creamy. Scrape into prepared pan. Refrigerate 3 hours or until firm. Cut into 1-inch squares. Store in refrigerator.

Yield: 64 pieces.

Candace is originally from Des Moines, Iowa. She developed her interest in entering contests from all the ribbons her cousins received through 4-H in the Iowa State Fair. She has been a resident of Arizona for over 30 years. She enjoys collecting recipes and cook books.

Prickly Pear Candy

Mark Soto — Glendale

1 cup prickly pear juice
1/2 cup water
1/8 tsp. salt

2 envelopes plain gelatin
2 cups sugar

Pick fruit using heavy rubber gloves. Singe off spines, wash and peel fruit. Mash pulp and put through 4 layers of cheesecloth.

Bring juice, water, sugar, and salt to a boil. Add gelatin to hot juice and stir until desolved. Boil slowly for 10 minutes. Pour into buttered 8-inch square pan. Allow to set for 15 hours. Cut candy into small squares and roll in powdered sugar.

Southern Pralines

Mary M. Sanderson — Mesa

2 cups granulated sugar
3/4 tsp. baking soda
1 cup light cream (half & half)

1 1/2 Tbsp. butter
2 cups pecan halves

Combine sugar and cream, let sit for about 30 minutes. Add baking soda and bring to a boil over medium heat, stirring constantly. Cook and stir to soft ball stage (234°). The mixture will slightly caramelize as it cooks. Remove from heat; add butter. Stir in pecans; beat long enough to drop from spoon (about 2 minutes). Blend in tablespoonful of hot water if mixture is too stiff. Drop by tablespoonfuls on wax paper.

Makes 2 dozen pralines.

Notes: Mixing the cream and sugar together gives a less granular candy. Watch mixture carefully when it begins to lose its gloss as it will stiffen quickly.

Holiday Pecan or Peanut Brittle

Carl Schwent — Phoenix

1 cup sugar
1/8 tsp. salt
1/2 cup light corn syrup
1/2 lb. raw peanuts or coarsely chopped pecans
    (approximately 1 1/2 cups)
1 Tbsp. butter or margarine
1 tsp. vanilla extract
1/2 Tbsp. baking soda

Grease a foil-lined cookie sheet with shortening or margarine. Mix sugar, salt, and corn syrup together in a 2 or 3-quart microwave-safe glass bowl or casserole (best is a 2-quart glass measuring cup with a handle). Fold in nuts.

Put in microwave and cook on high for 3 minutes. Stir with a heat-resistant spoon. Cook on high for 4 more minutes. Stir in butter. Continue cooking on high for 1 to 3 minutes or until syrup is light tan. Remove from microwave.

Add vanilla and baking soda. Stir briefly until the mixture foams and then pour out onto the greased cookie sheet. Be careful; the mixture and bowl will be very hot! Quickly spread out thin. When cool, break into small pieces and store in an airtight container.

Note: Microwave times are for a 600 to 700 watt microwave oven. Lower power ovens will take longer.

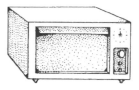

ARIZONA STATE FAIR

Blue Ribbon ™

BREAD RECIPES

Banana Nut
Breakfast Muffins

Karen Bulkeley — Phoenix

1/2 cup all-purpose flour (unsifted)
3/4 cup whole wheat flour (unsifted)
2 tsp. baking powder
1/2 tsp. salt
1 egg
1/4 cup melted butter or margarine
1/2 cup firmly packed brown sugar
1/2 cup milk
1 ripe banana
1 cup chopped pecans
1/2 tsp. cinnamon

In large bowl, stir together all-purpose flour, whole wheat flour, baking powder, and salt until thoroughly blended. Make a well in the center. In a separate bowl, lightly beat egg; stir in melted butter, brown sugar and milk. Mash banana by hand or in food processor and add to liquid ingredients. Add pecans to liquid ingredients. Pour liquid into flour well. Stir just enough to moisten all the dry ingredients. Spoon batter into greased muffin cups, filling each 2/3 full. Spinkle ***Cinnamon Nut Topping*** evenly on muffins.

Bake at 375° for about 25 minutes or until well browned and tops spring back when lightly touched. Makes about 9 muffins.

Cinnamon Nut Topping

4 Tbsp. packed brown sugar
4 Tbsp. chopped pecans
1 tsp. cinnamon

Mix together in small bowl and sprinkle on muffins.

Zucchini-Pineapple Bread

Norma Eakin — Chandler

1 cup oil
3 eggs
2 cups sugar
2 tsp. vanilla
2 cups shredded zucchini
   with skin

3 2/3 cups flour
1 tsp. salt
1 tsp. soda
1/2 tsp. baking powder
2 1/2 tsp. cinnamon

1 (20 oz.) can crushed pineapple, well drained

Mix together oil, eggs, sugar and vanilla. Add zucchini and pineapple. Blend all dry ingredients together and add to mixture. Blend well. Put into two (2) well greased and floured loaf pans. Bake at 350 degrees for about 1 hour. For variety, any of the following can be added: Nuts, maraschino cherries, chopped dates, raisins or chocolate chips.

12-Hour Rolls

Carol Cluff — Phoenix

1 pkg. yeast
1 cup sugar
1 cup luke warm water
1/2 cup butter or margarine

3 eggs, well beaten
1/2 tsp. salt
4 cups flour

Dissolve yeast and sugar in water. Melt butter and add to yeast mixture. Add eggs and salt. Add flour and mix well. Do not knead. Cover, let rise, leave until doubled. Divide into two parts. Turn out on floured board. Roll each part in a circle about 1/3" thick. Spread with butter. Cut in 16 slices like a pie. Roll up each slice starting with the large end. Let rise in pan and bake 10 minutes at 375°. Brush with melted butter when they come out of oven.

Honey-Pumpkin Gems

Mary Jane McHenry — Phoenix

2 cups all-purpose flour
1 Tbsp. baking powder
1 tsp. ground cinnamon
1/4 tsp. ground nutmeg
1/4 tsp. ground ginger
1/4 tsp. salt
1/2 cup canola oil
1/2 cup honey
2 large eggs
1 cup canned pumpkin
1/2 cup sour cream
2 (3 oz.) pkgs. cream cheese cut into 12 cubes
3 Tbsp. apricot preserves
1/4 cup sliced or chopped almonds

In a large bowl mix together flour, baking powder, cinnamon, nutmeg, ginger and salt. In another bowl, beat oil and honey until blended. Add the eggs, pumpkin and sour cream. Beat until thoroughly mixed. Stir pumpkin mixture into the dry ingredients just until moistened. Batter will be stiff.

Spoon batter into 12 paper-lined 2 1/2" muffin cups, filling halfway. Place 1 cheese cube in the center of each cup. Top cubes equally with preserves. Completely cover cheese and jam with remaining batter. Sprinkle muffin tops with almonds. Bake in a 400° oven until well browned, about 20-25 min. Remove from pan and cool at least 10 minutes. If made ahead, wrap airtight and chill until the next day. Freeze to store longer. Thaw wrapped. To reheat follow preceding directions.

Yields 12 muffins.

Raisin Bread

Rita Hutt — Mesa

1 3/4 cups milk
3/8 cup sugar
1/2 Tbsp. salt
6 Tbsp. margarine
1/2 cup very warm water
2 pkgs. active dry yeast
1/2 cup oat bran
6-6 1/2 cups unbleached flour
1 Tbsp. cinnamon
1 1/2 cups raisins

In small saucepan, heat milk just until bubbles form around edges. Remove from heat; add sugar, salt, and margarine; stir to melt margarine and let cool to lukewarm.

Sprinkle yeast over warm water (105° to 115°) in large bowl, stirring until yeast is dissolved. Stir in milk mixture. Add oat bran and blend thoroughly. Add half the flour; beat until smooth—about 2 minutes. Add the cinnamon and raisins. Then gradually add the remaining flour, mixing with hands until dough is stiff enough to leave sides of bowl.

Turn out dough onto lightly floured board. Cover with the bowl and let rest 10 minutes. Knead for about 10 minutes, or until dough is smooth and elastic.

Place dough in lightly greased large bowl, turning dough to bring up greased side. Cover with a towel and let rise in a warm place, free from drafts, for about 1 hour or until doubled in bulk. Punch down dough with fist, turn out onto lightly floured board, divide in half and shape each half into a smooth ball. Cover with towel and let rest 10 minutes. Shape each portion into a loaf; stretch the dough until it's about 25 inches long; fold over into thirds, then press in a 7" square; fold dough in thirds from the opposite direction to form a loaf shape; seal edge and ends of loaf

(Continued on next page)

(**Raisin Bread** continued)

by pinching; place seam-side down in two greased loaf pans.

Brush each loaf with melted margarine. Cover with towel and let rise in warm place, free from drafts, until double in bulk. When a finger poked into dough leaves an indentation, rising is sufficient.

Bake in preheated 375° oven for 35-40 minutes. Tops should be well browned and sound hollow when rapped with knuckles. Remove from pans immediately and cool on wire racks.

Note: If using mini-loaf pans, bake about 20 minutes.

Breakfast Cake

Gladys Messerschmidt — Phoenix

2 cups sugar
4 cups flour
4 Tbsp. baking powder

1 cup margarine
4 eggs, separated
1 1/2 cups milk

Combine sugar, flour and baking powder. Add margarine and mix to form crumbs. Set aside 1/2 cup crumbs. Add egg yolks and milk. Mix just till well moistened. Beat egg whites and fold into batter. Pour batter into 2 greased and floured 10" pie plates. Sprinkle the crumbs on top of batter in pans. Bake at 350° for 45 minutes. When done spoon 3 tablespoonfuls melted butter on top and sprinkle with cinnamon. Let cool. These freeze well.

This recipe is at least four generations old. The recipe was published in our small town newspaper in Pennsylvania Dutch Country, and has been a favorite of easy recipes in the family for a long time.

Honey
Cooking Soft Pretzels

Jill Heflin — Phoenix

1 pkg. active dry yeast
1 Tbsp. honey
1 cup warm water
2 1/2 to 3 cups all-purpose flour
1 tsp. salt
2 Tbsp. salad oil
1 egg white, beaten with 1 tsp. of each: salt and water
caraway seeds or coarse salt.

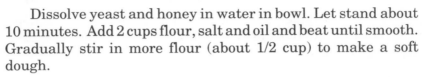

Dissolve yeast and honey in water in bowl. Let stand about 10 minutes. Add 2 cups flour, salt and oil and beat until smooth. Gradually stir in more flour (about 1/2 cup) to make a soft dough.

Turn dough onto a floured surface, knead until smooth and elastic, adding more flour (up to 1/2 cup) if necessary to prevent dough from being too sticky. Place dough in a greased bowl. Cover, let rise in a warm place until doubled, 45 minutes to 1 hour.

Punch dough down and divide into 12 equal balls. Roll each out with palms of hands, on floured surface, to form an 18-inch long rope. Twist into pretzel shapes, tucking ends under. Place on greased baking sheets. Let rise, uncovered, (until puffy) 20 to 25 minutes. Brush pretzels lightly with egg white mixture and sprinkle with caraway seeds or coarse salt. Bake at 425° until well browned (12 to 15 minutes). Cool slightly on wire racks; then serve warm.

Yields 12 pretzels

I am extremely honored to have my recipe published. I really enjoy entering things in the Arizona State Fair. I have entered in the State Fair since I was about 8 years old. I now have 3 children who are being raised with the same tradition.

Zucchini Bread

Ginny Greenhause — Glendale

2 cups sugar
1 cup oil
3 eggs
2 cups peeled & grated
    zucchini
3 tsp. vanilla

1 cup chopped nuts
3 cups flour
1 tsp. salt
3 tsp. cinnamon
1 tsp. soda
1/4 tsp. baking powder

Mix sugar, oil and eggs. Add zucchini, vanilla and nuts. Add flour, salt, cinnamon, soda and baking powder and mix well. Pour into greased and floured loaf pans. Place in a 350° oven for 50-60 minutes. Makes 2 large loaves.

Hint: To make this recipe easier, I usually put cut up zucchini into my blender with a little water, blend, and then sieve out the water.

Strawberry Nut Bread

Barbara Hummell — Phoenix

3 cups flour
1 tsp. salt
1 1/2 cups sugar
1/2 cup oil
2 cups (16 oz.) frozen
    strawberries (thawed)

1 tsp. baking soda
1 tsp. cinnamon
4 well beaten eggs
1/2 tsp. vanilla
2/3 cup chopped pecans

Blend all ingredients together and pour into 2 large greased and floured loaf pans or 3 (4" x 7") pans. Bake at 350° for 45 to 55 minutes. Check with toothpick to be sure bread is done in center. Let cool on wire rack before removing from pans.

100% Whole Wheat Bread

Julie McFarland — Mesa

5 cups warm water
10 1/2 cups whole wheat flour
2/3 cup honey
2/3 cup oil
2/3 cup gluten flour
1/4 tsp. vitamin C crystals
    (citric acid)
3 Tbsp. yeast (Saf-instant®) or
    any instant yeast
1 Tbsp. salt

Mix water (warmed to 110°) with 3 cups of flour then add rest of ingredients. When adding the yeast, be careful to sprinkle it in the bread mixture a little at a time so it has time to dissolve into the wet ingredients. (There is no need to proof your yeast if you are using instant.) Add the rest of the flour one cup at a time until the dough pulls away from the sides of the mixing bowl. Be sure to not add too much flour or your bread will be too dry.

Mix on high for 5 to 7 minutes. While your bread is mixing, spray 4 bread pans with Pam® cooking spray.

After mixing is done, pour dough onto oiled surface and cut into 4 equal parts. Shape your bread into loafs and place in individual bread pans and let rise until double in size. There is no need to let your bread dough rise twice if you are using instant yeast.

Bake at 325° for 25 to 35 minutes or till golden brown.

Note: I use a Bosch® machine. Any machine that has a good motor and dough hook should work great. If this recipe is made by hand, you will need to let it rise once in a large greased bowl and then again in your bread pans.

Yeast Rolls

Simon C. Krevitsky — Phoenix

4 cups milk
1 cup sugar
4 tsp. salt
4 yeast cakes
4 eggs
1 cup shortening
14 to 15 cups flour
beaten egg
poppy seeds (optional)

Mix together four cups luke warm milk, sugar and salt. Crumble yeast cakes into mixture. Stir until yeast is dissolved. Stir in eggs. Mix in shortening with hands. Add five cups of flour and mix until well blended. Add five more cups of flour and gradually add additional flour in 1/2 cup increments until dough becomes glossy and elastic. Turn dough into greased bowl and grease the top of the dough. Cover with damp cloth and keep in a warm 80° room that is draft free.

Let dough rise 1 1/2 to 2 hours until it is almost double in size. Press two fingers into dough. It will leave indentations when dough is doubled.

Punch down the dough by thrusting fist into dough, pull edges into center and turn completely over in bowl. Let it rise again until it is almost double in bulk (30 to 45 minutes).

After second rising, divide the dough into 4 equal sections. Round up, cover and let rest for 15 minutes so dough is easy to handle.

From this point on you may shape your rolls any way you like. Brush them with egg before baking and sprinkle on poppy seeds if you like. Cover the rolls and let them rise about an hour before baking. Bake at 375° until they are golden brown.

Yields about 6 doz. small rolls.

"Give-it-a-try" Gingerbread

Bonita Ruiz — Phoenix

1 3/4 cups unbleached flour
1 tsp. baking soda
1/2 tsp. ground cinnamon
1/4 tsp. salt
1 tsp. ground ginger
1/3 cup shortening

1/2 cup granulated sugar
1 large egg
1/2 cup unsulphured
    molasses
2/3 cup hot water

Preheat oven to 350°. Grease an 8 x 8 x 2 baking pan. In a large bowl, whisk together first 5 ingredients. In another bowl, cream the shortening and sugar. Add egg and half of the flour mixture to creamed mixture. Blend thoroughly. Add balance of flour mixture, molasses and 1/3 cup of hot water, blending thoroughly after adding each addtion. Add the second 1/3 cup of water and blend thoroughly.

Pour and scrape into the baking pan using a spatula to push the batter into the corners of the pan. Bake at 350° for 30 minutes, or until the cake springs back when lightly touched in the center. When done serve while warm right out of the pan or turn out onto a plate and serve with confectioners' sugar sprinkled over the top or with big dollop of fresh whipped cream.

Baking Powder Biscuits

Pearl L. Erwin — Phoenix

2 cups sifted flour
2 tsp. sugar
4 tsp. baking powder
1/2 tsp. salt

1/2 tsp. cream of tartar
1/2 cup shortening
2/3 cup milk

Combine dry ingredients. Cut in shortening, then add milk and stir lightly. Place on floured board and roll about 1/2 inch thick and cut desired size. Bake at 450° for 10 to 12 minutes.

Amish Friendship Bread

Lisa Reeves — Scottsdale

Starter

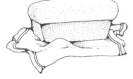

Day 1:
   2 cups unbleached flour
   2 cups warm water
   1 pkg. dry yeast

Using a large glass or ceramic bowl and wooden or plastic spoon only, combine ingredients. Stir well, (might be slightly lumpy) and leave uncovered.

Days 2, 3, 4: Stir well

Day 5: Feed starter with **1 cup milk, 1 cup sugar,** and **1 cup flour.** Stir well.

Days 6-9: Stir well.

Day 10: Feed starter with **1 cup milk, 1 cup sugar, 1 cup flour.** Stir well! Divide starter into four (4) separate batches (1 cup each). Keep one for yourself. Give two to two of your friends.

To the remaining batter add:

2/3 cup oil (or 1/3 cup
   applesauce and 1/3 cup oil)
1 cup sugar
2 cups flour
1 1/4 tsp. baking powder

3 eggs
1/2 tsp. cinnamon
1/2 tsp. vanilla
1/4 tsp. salt
1/2 tsp. baking soda

Mix all ingredients well. Pour into two well-greased (I prefer a cooking spray) and sugared 8 1/2 x 4 1/2 loaf pans. Bake 350° for 50 to 55 minutes. Cool 10 minutes before removing from pans.

You may add any of the following ingredients for a different flavor: Dried fruit, fresh fruit, nuts, raisins, 1 cup applesauce, cherries, coconut, heath bits, raisins, poppy seeds etc.

(Continued on next page)

(**Amish Friendship Bread** continued)

Special note: If using canned fruit, i.e. peaches or pineapple, drain extremely well. (Don't use applesauce instead of oil.) Also, if you would like to keep one starter, put it in a covered container and freeze until ready to use. When ready to use, start at day 1 and begin.

This recipe has been going on with family and friends for over 5 years!

100% Whole Wheat Bread

Peggy Bechtle — Glendale

6 cups hot water
2/3 cup honey
3 Tbsp. yeast
3 Tbsp. dough-enhancer powder*

2/3 cup canola oil
2 Tbsp. salt
12-14 cups whole wheat flour (or more, as needed)

Combine all ingredients in the bowl of a heavy-duty electric mixer (with 500-700 watt motor. Or it can be mixed by hand, but then will require two risings.) Add enough whole-wheat flour until mixture cleans sides of bowl. Knead 8-10 minutes, then check texture to see if gluten is well-developed. Cut dough into 5 large pieces. Form into loaves and put in greased 9 x 5 x 3 loaf pans. Let rise until nicely rounded on top, 20-30 minutes. Bake at 350° for 25 minutes. Makes 5 loaves.

*Available at baking supply shops.

Sticky Pecan
Sweet Rolls

Eunice Moore — Phoenix

1/2 cup oil	2 pkgs. dry yeast
1/2 cup sugar	6 cups flour
2 eggs	1 Tbsp. salt
2 cups warm water	

Using a large mixer, blend oil and sugar, and then add eggs. Mix together water and yeast till yeast is dissolved. Add to egg mixture. Combine flour and salt. Add 4 cups of flour mixture to the egg mixture and mix until the dough is very smooth (approximately 5 minutes with dough hook). Slowly add remaining flour. (May not need all the flour. Just add enough for dough to be easy to handle for kneading.) Knead until smooth. Place dough in well greased large bowl. (I spray plastic wrap with Pam®, and lay it loosely on top of dough.) Cover the dough lightly with a soft tea towel and place the bowl in warm place to rise until doubled.

On a lightly floured counter top, punch down and divide dough into thirds. Roll each third into a rectangle using rolling pin. Spread dough with **soft butter,** sprinkle with about **1/3 cup sugar.** Sprinkle with **cinnamon** to taste. Roll up dough along the long side and pinch to seal. With sharp knife cut into pieces about 1 1/2 inches wide. Put in three 8" round prepared pans to rise till double in size. (To prepare pans: butter bottoms, sprinkle with brown sugar, dot with butter, and then drizzle with **white corn syrup.** Distribute generous quantity of **pecans** in each.) Lightly cover and let rise in warm place. Bake in 350° oven about 20 to 25 minutes or till golden brown. Turn out on waxed paper.

Powdered Sugar Frosting

1 1/2 cups powdered sugar	dash of salt
1 tsp. vanilla	4 Tbsp. butter

Combine ingredients in small bowl. Add enough **milk** to bring mixture to spreading consistency. Spread frosting on rolls when cooled.

Coconut Bread

Dorothy Neal — Phoenix

4 eggs
2 cups sugar
1 cup oil
2 tsp. coconut flavoring
3 cups flour
1/2 tsp. salt

1/2 tsp. baking soda
1/2 tsp. baking powder
1 cup buttermilk
1 cup nuts
1 cup coconut

Mix eggs, sugar and oil. Add coconut flavoring. To the flour add salt, baking soda and baking powder. Add to egg mixture, alternating with buttermilk. Add nuts and coconut. Put in a greased Bundt pan or 5 small loaf pans. Bake 1 hour at 325°. Pour glaze over cake while still hot and in the pan. Leave in pan 4 hours.

Glaze

1 1/2 cups sugar
3/4 cup water

3 Tbsp. butter
1 tsp. coconut flavoring

Boil for 5 minutes. Add 1 tsp. coconut flavoring. Stir, and pour over cake.

I love cooking and have compiled four small cook books with some recipes from my travels in France, Spain, Italy, Mexico and New York, and also from the places I have lived. I have had some of my recipes published in the paper. I am 76 years old.

Lorraine Wagner's Great Falls Pumpkin Bread

Linda Swain — Phoenix

3 cups white sugar
1 cup vegetable oil
4 eggs
2 cups canned pumpkin
2 tsp. cloves
2 tsp. nutmeg
2 tsp. cinnamon
3 1/3 cups white flour
1 tsp. baking powder
2 tsp. baking soda
1 1/2 tsp. salt

Heat oven to 325°. Grease three 8 1/2 x 4 1/2 x 2 1/2 loaf pans. In large mixing bowl, beat sugar and oil. Beat in eggs, pumpkin and spices. Blend in flour, baking powder, baking soda, and salt. Pour mixture into loaf pans.

Bake 60 to 70 minutes or until a toothpick inserted in center comes out clean.

Mom's Date Bread

Karen Osborne — Scottsdale

3 cups flour
2 tsp. baking soda
2 tsp. baking powder
1/4 tsp. salt
1/4 cup shortening
2 cups sugar

2 eggs
1 1/2 tsp. vanilla
1/2 cup chopped nuts
1 1/2 cups chopped dates
1 3/4 cups hot coffee

Sift flour, baking powder, baking soda, and salt together. Cream shortening adding sugar gradually. Mix well. Add beaten eggs and vanilla. Beat thoroughly. Mix dates and nuts with sifted dry ingredients and add to moist ingredients alternately with coffee. Lightly grease two 4 1/2 x 8 1/2 pans. Then cut out a piece of waxed paper to fit in the bottom of the pans. Lightly grease the paper. Pour the mixture into the loaf pans. Let stand for 15 minutes. Bake in moderate 350° oven for 35 to 40 minutes. When bread is done, turn it over immediately and pull off the waxed paper. Then, turn it over and wrap in foil immediately, so the crust will stay soft. Remove the foil when the bread has cooled.

Boston Brown Bread

Diana Prahl — Green Valley

1 1/2 cups seedless raisins
1 1/2 cups boiling water
1 cup sugar
3 Tbsp. margarine
1 egg

2 3/4 cups sifted flour
2 tsp. baking soda
1/2 tsp. salt
1 tsp. vanilla
1 cup nuts

Place raisins in boiling water and simmer for 3 minutes. Set them aside to cool. Cream sugar and margarine. Add egg, raisins and water mixture. Mix in flour, soda, salt, vanilla and nuts. Grease and flour 4 tin cans (# 2 size). Fill cans 1/2 full. Bake at 350° for 45 minutes. Cool in cans for 5 minutes; then remove to cool on racks.

Tea Scones

Mary Lindsay Sanderson — Mesa

2 cups unbleached and unsifted flour
2 1/2 tsp. baking powder
1/2 tsp. salt
1/4 cup sifted confectioners' sugar
6 Tbsp. cold butter, cut up
2 Tbsp. currants or raisins
1 egg beaten with enough half & half cream
    for 2/3 cup liquid (save 1 Tbsp. for tops of scones)

Mix all dry ingredients in bowl and cut in butter. Add dry fruit.

Mix in the egg/cream mixture with a fork. Dough will be slightly sticky. Turn into a lightly floured surface and knead 5 to 6 turns. Pat out to 1/2 inch with fingers and cut into 2-inch rounds or triangles. Brush tops with reserved egg mixture. Place on lightly floured baking sheet and bake in preheated oven at 425° for approximately 15 minutes until risen and nicely browned on top.

Mary was born and raised in Scotland and has lived in Mesa for 21 years. Mary and her husband travel to Scotland frequently and both are interested in promoting their Scottish heritage through several organizations in Arizona and the United States.

Mary's grandmother was a good baker and told her to always have "a light hand" with pastry and scones. Scones should be mixed and baked quickly.

Bagels

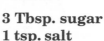

Veronica Sadler — Peoria

4 1/2 cups flour
2 pkgs. yeast
1 1/2 cups warm water
3 Tbsp. sugar
1 tsp. salt

Combine 1 1/2 cups of the flour with the yeast. Mix water, sugar, and salt. Beat 1/2 minute at low speed and 3 minutes at high speed. With your hands, stir in enough of the flour to make moderately stiff dough. Turn onto floured surface and knead till smooth and elastic (8 to 10 minutes). Cover and let rest 15 minutes. Cut into 12 portions, shape into balls, and punch a hole in center of each. Pull gently to enlarge hole. Cover and let rise 20 minutes. Combine **1 Tbsp. sugar** and **1 gallon water** in a large kettle. Bring to boil. Reduce to simmer; cook 4 or 5 bagels at a time for 7 minutes, turning once. Drain and place on greased baking sheet. Bake at 375° for 30-35 minutes.

Yields 12 bagels

Herb Bread

Lettie L. Zenor — Phoenix

2 1/4 cups bread flour
2 Tbsp. sugar
1 Tbsp. powdered milk
1 tsp. salt
1 Tbsp. butter
2 Tbsp. parsley flakes
1 Tbsp. caraway seeds
1 Tbsp. (1/2 dill weed, 1/2 dill seed)
15/16 cup water
1 tsp. dry yeast

Mix and bake by your bread machine directions. *I use light color setting.

I bake three or four loaves of various breads each week and very seldom buy bakery bread. I enjoy trying different varieties of bread recipes and enjoy the competition at State Fair time.

Best Ever
Banana Bread

Dianna Stolba — Glendale

1 3/4 cups flour
1 1/2 cups sugar
1 tsp. soda
1/2 tsp. salt
2 eggs
2 ripe bananas,
    mashed (1 cup)
1/2 cup oil

1/4 cup plus 1 Tbsp.
    buttermilk
1 tsp. vanilla
1 cup chopped nuts
1/2 cup chocolate
    chips (optional)
1 Tbsp. flour

In a large bowl, stir together flour, sugar, soda and salt.

In another bowl, combine eggs, bananas, oil, buttermilk and vanilla. Add flour mixture, stirring until just combined. Stir in nuts. If adding chocolate chips, combine with flour and add at this time. Pour into a greased 9 x 5 x 3 loaf pan.

Bake at 325° for 1 hour and 20 minutes or until bread tests done. Cool on wire rack.

Note: Recipe does not double well.

Tip: Dusting the chocolate chips with flour helps suspend the chips in the mixture so they won't settle on the bottom of the pan.

Velvety Crumb
Swedish Rye Bread

Stan Strom — Gilbert

2 packages quick-rise yeast	1/3 cup shortening
1/2 cup warm water	2 tsp. salt
2 Tbsp. sugar	2 cups boiling water
2 cups sifted rye flour	3 or 4 cups sifted
3/4 cup dark molasses	white flour

Soften dry yeast in warm water (105 to 115°) with sugar (to activate yeast) about 10 minutes before mixing other ingredients. A mushroom top may appear. Combine rye flour, molasses, shortening and salt. Add boiling water and blend well. (It's easier if you have an Osterizer® with bread kneading hooks.) Allow to cool slightly before adding softened yeast mixture. Gradually stir in white flour to make soft dough or just enough so hands don't stick. Mix well. Turn out on a well floured surface, cover with cloth or towel and let rest 10 minutes. Knead dough until smooth and satiny (usually 10 minutes by hand or less if using a bread kneading machine). Place in lightly greased bowl, turning once to grease top surface. Cover and let rise in warm place until double in size. (I usually take out top oven rack, turn on at 200° for 5 minutes, then turn oven off and put bowl of dough on lower rack for 1 to 1 1/2 hours.) Punch down. Cover and let rise again until double.

Turn out on floured surface and divide into three balls. Cover for 15 minutes. Shape into round loaves and place on greased baking sheet or in pie tins. (You may also shape loaves to fit greased bread pans). Cover until double in size (1 hour). For a shiny crust: brush loaves with one egg yolk mixed with 1 tsp. water before baking. For a sheen crust: brush loaves with one egg white mixed with 1 tsp. water before baking. Bake in 350° oven for 35-40 minutes. Cool and then transfer to a wire rack.

Note: This is a delicious, dark, rich and moist bread with a robust flavor.

Flour Tortillas

Vicki Vasquez — Higley

3 cups LaPina® brand flour
1/4 cup lard
1 1/2 tsp. baking powder
1 1/2 tsp. salt
1 to 1 1/2 cups warm water

In a food processor with chopping blade, place flour, lard, salt, and baking powder. Mix until lard is completely incorporated. While mixing, slowly trickle in enough water until there is one ball of dough. It should be firm like your ear lobe. Form into 20 balls and place in a shallow sealed container. Heat a heavy cast iron skillet on medium-high heat until a drop of water dances on the surface (like pancakes).

Line the sealed container that you are going to put the tortillas in with a dish towel to absorb the heat moisture. As you roll out the dough, lightly pat with flour to keep from sticking to counter or rolling pin. Roll until you have a 10-inch circle. Place on hot griddle. When it has brown spots, turn over and cook on the other side (cook about 30 seconds on each side). Place in the towel lined container. Repeat until done.

Makes about 20 tortillas.

While there are just a few ingredients, the trick to great tortillas is in the method. With practice they only get better.

PIE RECIPES

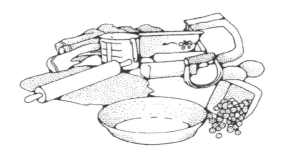

Cherry-Apple Pie

Patricia A. Belford — Phoenix

Special Crust:

1/2 tsp. baking powder	2/3 cup shortening
2 cups flour	1 egg
1/4 tsp. salt	1/4 cup water
2 Tbsp. sugar	1 tsp. vinegar
1 tsp. apple pie spice or cinnamon	

Sift dry ingredients together; cut in shortening till cornmeal texture. Mix egg, water, and vinegar together and add to flour mixture. Mix to form a ball and divide into two crusts.

Cherry-Apple Pie Filling

20 oz. can cherry pie filling	1/4 tsp. nutmeg
1/4 tsp. mace	1 tsp. cinnamon
2 Tbsp. dark brown sugar	1 Tbsp. butter
pinch of salt	
2 1/2 to 3 lbs. pippin, Granny Smith or other tart apple	

Peel, core and thinly slice the apples. Mix all ingredients together and place in a deep dish pie pan that has been lined with the special crust. Be creative with your lattice work top. Brush crust with an egg and water mixture to achieve a glossy golden crust.

Bake at 425° for 10 minutes; reduce heat to 350° and continue baking 25-35 minutes until golden brown.

Our Cherry-Apple Pie is our own invention out of necessity. Dad doesn't like apple pie; we do. However, we all like cherries and the cherry-apple combination.

Apple Pie

Dianna Bennett — Phoenix

2 cups sifted all-purpose flour
6 to 7 Tbsp. cold water
2/3 cup Butter Flavor Crisco®
1 tsp. salt

Cut shortening into flour, add 6 to 7 tablespoons of cold water and salt to mixture. Mix with hands only till mixture is sticky. Roll out into two crusts and put one into a 9" pie pan.

3 lbs. Granny Smith apples
1 cup sugar
1 1/2 tsp. cinnamon
1 tsp. nutmeg
3 Tbsp. flour

Peel, core and slice apples; mix in sugar, cinnamon and nutmeg. Sprinkle flour over apples as you layer them into the pie crust. Add top crust; seal, score and brush with egg whites. Bake 50 minutes at 350°.

My pie recipe came from two of my grandmothers. I learned how to sweeten the apples from my great-grandmother Agnes, who was famous throughout the family for her pies.

As in any pie, the crust for my pie is the special part. My dad's mother taught me in the summer of 1986, just how to prepare the dough to make the flakiest crust ever. With a combination of the two I came up with this prize winning recipe that I hope to pass on to my own daughter.

Lemon Meringue Pie

Mary Ann Butler — Phoenix

1 cup sugar
1 1/2 cups cold water
1/4 cup lemon juice,
   plus 2 Tbsp. (tart)

1/4 cup cornstarch
3 egg yolks, slightly beaten
1 Tbsp. margarine
1 baked pie crust

In double boiler combine sugar and cornstarch. Using whisk, gradually stir in water until smooth. Stir in slightly beaten egg yolks. Stirring constantly, bring to boil; boil until thick. Remove from heat, stir in juice and margarine. Pour into baked **Pie Crust** and top with **Meringue.**

Meringue

3 egg whites
1/8 tsp. cream tartar

1/3 cup sugar

In small mixing bowl beat egg whites at high speed until foamy. Add cream of tartar. Gradually add sugar until stiff peaks form. Spread meringue over hot filling, sealing to the edges. Bake in 350° oven 15 to 20 minutes or till golden brown. Cool on rack; then refrigerate. Makes 6 to 8 servings.

Pie Crust

2 cups sifted all-purpose flour
2/3 cup shortening

1 tsp. salt
5 to 6 Tbsp. cold water

In a bowl, combine shortening with flour and salt and mix until crumbly. Add water gradually till pastry forms a soft ball (not sticky). Divide into 2 balls and roll out on pastry sheet or floured board. Makes 2 (8" to 9") crusts.

Bake crust at 450° for 6 to 8 minutes or until golden brown; watch carefully.

Note: I use Butter Flavor Crisco®.

Peach Pie

Therese M. Clark — Tucson

3 cups flour	1 cup shortening
1 tsp. baking powder	ice cold water to mix
1 tsp. salt	

Sift together the flour, salt and baking powder. Work in the shortening with a fork and mix to a firm dough with the ice-cold water. Divide into two parts and roll out each crust on floured board.

5 cups sliced fresh peaches	2 Tbsp. tapioca or flour
3/4 cup sugar	1/4 tsp. salt

Mix all ingredients well and let stand for several hours. Pour into pastry lined (9-inch) pie pan. Dot with little dabs of margarine. Top with pastry. Sprinkle cinnamon sugar across top. Bake at 425° for 15 minutes, then 350° for 45 minutes.

Note: The peach filling can be made ahead of time and frozen if you add 1 tsp. of Fruit Fresh® to the mix. Be sure all peaches are coated with the sugar/flour/tapioca/etc. mix.

Pecan Pie

Alice Gehlbach — Glendale

3 eggs	1 cup corn syrup
1 cup sugar	2 Tbsp. butter
salt	1 to 2 tsp. vanilla
1 1/2 cups pecans	1 unbaked pie crust

Stir together eggs, corn syrup, sugar, butter, salt, and vanilla. Cook over medium heat just until mixture boils. Remove from heat; add pecans. Pour into unbaked pie crust. Bake in 350° oven for 50 minutes.

Pumpkin Pie

Kim Cummings — Scottsdale

4 eggs
2 cups fresh pumpkin
1 1/2 cups sugar
2 tsp. salt
2 tsp. ground cinnamon

1 tsp. ground ginger
1/2 tsp. ground cloves
1 can sweetened
    condensed milk

Prepare 2 unbaked 9" deep dish pie shells. Preheat oven to 375°. In a large bowl lightly beat eggs. Add all other ingredients and mix. Fill shells and bake 70 minutes or until a toothpick tests clean.

Fresh pumpkin is the secret in this recipe. Wash and slice a medium size ripe pumpkin into 3 wedges. Remove the outer orange skin with a potato peeler. Dice and steam till tender. Cool, beat and drain off excess liquid. Fresh pumpkin creates a much heartier, juicier flavor and provides an appealing color with incredible fluffiness.

Good things come to those who wait. If you have the patience and time to prepare my recipe from fresh pumpkin, your pie will become the star of your Thanksgiving dinner and outshine any turkey!

Sour Cream Lemon Pie

Lucille Koch — Sun City

1 baked (9") pie shell
1 cup sugar
3 Tbsp. cornstarch
1/4 cup butter
1 Tbsp. grated lemon rind

1/4 cup lemon juice
3 egg yolks
1 cup milk
1 cup sour cream

In a saucepan combine sugar and cornstarch; add butter, lemon rind and juice. Beat in egg yolks, stir in milk and cook over medium heat, stirring constantly until thickened. Cool. Pour in sour cream. Spoon into pie shell and chill for 2 hours. Garnish with whipped cream and chopped nuts (optional).

Strawberry Rhubarb Pie

Lowell B. Ebrite — Phoenix

1 cup sugar
1/4 tsp. salt
1/4 tsp. nutmeg
2 Tbsp. quick cooking tapioca
1/4 cup orange juice
3 cups cut rhubarb
1 Orange Pastry Crust*
1 cup sliced strawberries
1 Tbsp. butter

Combine sugar, salt, nutmeg, tapioca, orange juice, and rhubarb. Place in 9-inch pie pan lined with Orange Pastry Crust. Top with strawberries and dot with butter. Adjust top crust. Bake in hot oven (450°) 10 minutes, then in moderate oven (350°) for 30 minutes.

*For Orange Pastry Crust, add 1 Tbsp. grated orange peel to **Plain Pastry Crust**.

Plain Pastry Crust
(for 8 or 9-inch double crust pie)

1 1/2 cups flour
1/2 tsp. salt
1/2 cup shortening
4 to 5 Tbsp. cold water

Sift flour and salt; add shortening. Cut in with pastry blender or blending fork until the pieces are the size of small peas. Add cold water by teaspoonfuls, tossing with a fork until all the flour coated bits of fat are barely dampened. Stop! Turn mixture onto a square of waxed paper. Gather corners, pressing from the outside to form a compact ball.

Divide for lower and upper crust. Chill for easier handling.

Raisin Pie

(Funeral Pie)

Rhea J. Jacanin — Phoenix

1 1/2 cups raisins (uncooked)
1/2 cup (firmly packed) brown sugar
1/4 tsp. salt
2 tsp. vanilla
1 3/4 cups light corn syrup
3 eggs beaten
1 to 2 Tbsp. apricot brandy (optional)

Prepare 2 pie crusts. (Top is lattice style).

Heat oven to 425°. Mix all ingredients well and pour into pie shell. As you put on each piece of the top crust lattice, twist it once or twice to get a nice effect.

Bake at 425° for 10 minutes. Then reduce heat to 350°. Bake an additional 25 to 35 minutes. Before the last 20 minutes, put strips of foil around edges of crust to avoid over-browning.

Additions: try adding 1/4 cup of walnuts to mix before you bake or substitute orange peel for the apricot brandy if you prefer.

My grandmother used to call this "funeral pie". This pie always seemed to be at funerals when I was a child, especially in the winter when the fresh fruit supply was low. Hope you like it!

Apple Pie

Jane Nacinovich — Phoenix

3 cups sifted all-purpose flour
1 tsp. baking powder
1 1/8 tsp. salt
2 tsp. sugar
1/2 cup cold butter (cut in pieces)
1/2 cup cold shortening (freeze the day before and cut
    in pieces before you use it)
1/2 cup cold milk

Gently blend dry ingredients. With pastry blender cut cold, firm butter and shortening into dry ingredients until mixture looks like fine cornmeal. Add cold milk, a little at a time, over different parts of mixture, tossing quickly with a fork until all particles cling together when pressure is used. Divide dough using a bit more for bottom crust. Roll dough between 2 pieces of plastic wrap. Dampen kitchen counter with a clean moist dish cloth. Lay plastic wrap on surface. (If plastic wrap slides, your counter is too damp.) Roll out to about 12" in diameter. Gently remove top plastic wrap. Turn pie dough upside down and ease the dough into the pie plate, as pie dough shrinks when baked. Carefully remove top plastic wrap by keeping the wrap low to the dough. Do not lift upward. Place pie plate in the refrigerator.

Top Crust: Using the same method roll out top pie crust to desired size. Carefully remove top plastic wrap and cut decorative design into the top pie dough with a spoon. (Do not cut too close to the sides.) Place top pie crust in the refrigerator and begin the apple filling. Remove pie plate and top pie crust one-half hour before finishing the filling.

(Continued next page)

(*Apple Pie* continued)

Apple Pie Filling

5-6 medium to large Golden
    Delicious or Jonathan apples
1 1/2 cups sugar
4 Tbsp. flour
Adjust to taste:
    3/4 tsp. cinnamon
    1/4 tsp. nutmeg
2 tsp. vanilla
2 Tbsp. fresh or container orange juice

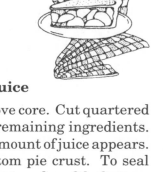

Peel apples; cut into quarters. Remove core. Cut quartered apples width wise, then add (in order) remaining ingredients. Mix well with large spoon until a small amount of juice appears. Place apple filling in the prepared bottom pie crust. To seal bottom and top crust, coat the top of the outer edge of the bottom crust with milk, rubbing over area a few times. Turn top crust upside down on apples, removing plastic wrap carefully. Do not stretch dough. Mark outer edge with a fork and cut away excess dough. Press around pie plate edge, pushing slightly inward to create a decorative edge. Lightly apply milk with fingers or brush to top crust. Sprinkle generously with sugar for a nice brown shiny crust.

Bake at 400° for glass pie plate, 425° for metal pie pan, for 50 minutes. Helpful hint: cover edge of crust with foil and bake for 40 minutes, remove foil and continue baking for 10 minutes. Cool on a wire rack.

Pumpkin Pie

Nancy Schaefer — Phoenix

1 1/2 cups canned pumpkin
3/4 cup sugar
1/2 tsp. salt
1 1/4 tsp. ground cinnamon
1/2 tsp. ground ginger
1/2 tsp. ground nutmeg
3 slightly beaten eggs
1 1/4 cups milk or cream or half and half
1 (6 oz.) can or 2/3 cup of evaporated milk
1 (9") unbaked pastry shell

Preheat oven to 400° Combine pumpkin, sugar, salt and spices.   Blend in eggs, milk and evaporated milk. Pour into pastry shell.

Bake at 400° for 50 minutes, or until knife inserted in center edge out clean. Cover crimped edges during baking if too much browning occurs.

Pie Crust

1 1/2 cups sifted all-purpose flour
1/2 tsp. salt
1/2 cup shortening
4 to 5 Tbsp. cold water

Sift flour and salt together; cut in shortening with pastry blender until pieces are the size of small peas. Sprinkle 1 Tbsp water over part of mixture. Gently toss with fork and push to the side. Repeat until all dough is moistened. Form into a ball. Flatten on lightly floured surface by pressing with edge of hand 3 times across in both directions. Roll from center to edge until 1/8" thick. Place in greased pie plate and crimp edges.

For a festive holiday appearance, cut maple leaves from pastry dough, bake separately and place on pumpkin pie after pie is completed.

Arizona's
Supreme Citrus Pie

Beth Sternitzky — Apache Junction

Prepare and bake your favorite pie crust in 9 or 9 1/2-inch deep dish pie plate. Cool completely.

Fluffy Filling

1 package (8 oz.) cream cheese, softened
1 can (14 oz.) sweetened condensed milk
1 can (6 oz.) frozen lemonade concentrate, thawed
1 package (4 serving size) lemon flavor instant
    pudding and pie filling mix (not sugar free)
1 cup whipping cream, whipped

Combine cream cheese and sweetened condensed milk in large bowl. Beat at low speed of electric mixer until smooth. Add lemonade concentrate. Blend well. Beat in pudding mix until smooth. Fold in whipped cream. Spoon into baked pie crust. Make shallow depression in filling 1 inch in from edge. Refrigerate.

Clear Filling

1/2 cup cornstarch	**1 1/2 cups granulated sugar**
1/3 cup water	**1 1/2 cups water**
4 egg yolks	**1 Tbsp. butter or margarine**
1/2 cup fresh lemon juice	

Combine cornstarch and 1/3 cup water in small bowl. Stir to blend. Combine egg yolks and lemon juice in medium bowl. Beat until smooth. Combine granulated sugar and remaining water in medium saucepan. Cook on medium heat until mixture comes to a boil. Stir in cornstarch mixture slowly. Cook and stir until thickened and clear. Remove from heat. Stir in egg yolk mixture slowly until blended. Return to heat.

(Continued on next page)

Cook and stir 1 to 2 minutes or until mixture comes to a boil. Remove from heat. Stir in butter until blended. Cool completely. Spread gently over fluffy filling.

Topping

1 cup whipping cream   **3/4 tsp. vanilla**
2 Tbsp. confectioners' sugar

For topping, beat whipping cream in small bowl at high speed of electric mixer until stiff peaks form. Beat in confectioners sugar and vanilla. Spread over clear filling. Refrigerate until firm.

Beth represented the State of Arizona with this pie, winning runner-up in the 1990 National Crisco American Pie Celebration.

Terry Cherry Pie

Kathy Bradshaw — Mesa

2 eggs   **2 cups flour**
1 tsp. salt   **1 cup shortening**

Beat eggs in a bowl and pour into measuring cup. Add cold water to bring to 1/2 cup. Mix well. Mix flour, salt, and shortening with pastry blender. Add egg mixture. Roll out pastry for two pie pans. Bake at 425° for 12 minutes. Watch closely. Cool.

1 can condensed milk   **1 tsp. vanilla**
1/3 cup pure lemon juice   **1/2 cup whipped cream**
1/2 tsp. almond extract   **1 can cherry pie filling**

Mix milk, lemon juice, almond extract and vanilla. Fold in whipped cream. Pour into pie shells. Chill 2 hours. Pour cherry filling on top. Chill until used.

Caramel Crunch
Pecan Pie

Marion Tipton — Phoenix

Make the **Toffee** and **Caramel Sauce** first.

Toffee

2 cups (firmly packed) dark brown sugar
1 Tbsp. cider vinegar
pinch of salt
1/4 cup salt free butter
2 Tbsp. boiling water
Butter Flavor Crisco®

Grease jellyroll pan with Butter Flavor Crisco. Combine first four ingredients with boiling water in a 3-quart (heavy) pot, stirring to blend well. Dissolve sugar over moderate heat and stir while mixture comes to a boil. Cover and let boil for 2 to 3 minutes. Uncover and wash down sides of pot with pastry brush dipped in cold water. Boil slowly until candy thermometer reaches hard-crack stage. Continue to stir gently without touching the sides of the pot. Pour into the jelly roll pan, let cool partially, then break up into small bits to sprinkle over top of caramel on top of pie. (Makes 3 - 4 tablespoonfuls.) Reserve rest for eating.

Caramel Sauce

2/3 cup sugar
1/3 cup water
1/2 cup plus 1 Tbsp. whipping cream (not whipped)
1/4 cup unsalted butter

Heat sugar and water in small (heavy) saucepan, over low heat. Stir until sugar dissolves. Increase heat to medium and boil, without stirring, until mixture is deep amber, brushing down sugar crystals from sides of pan with wet pastry brush (about 11 minutes). Remove from heat and add cream (mixture

(Continued on next page)

(*Caramel Crunch Pecan Pie* continued from previous page)

will bubble up). Add butter and stir until smooth.
Stir over low heat until color deepens and caramel thickens
slightly, about 3 minutes. Let cool at room temperature until
you are ready to use it on the pie. At this point prepare one
single 9" pie crust.

Caramel Crunch Pecan Filling

1 Tbsp. butter melted	1/2 tsp. salt
1 tsp. unsulphured molasses	3/4 cup sugar
1 Tbsp. Mrs. Butterworth's®	2 tsp. vanilla
Syrup	3 eggs
1 cup dark Karo® syrup	1 cup pecan pieces

Put first 8 ingredients into medium-sized mixing bowl and
whisk until well blended. Add pecan pieces. Stir well and pour
into unbaked pie shell that you have removed from freezer.
Bake for 10 minutes in preheated 400° oven and reduce heat to
350° and continue to bake for 25 more minutes.

Protect pie with foil while baking if crust seems to be getting
too brown. Remove pie from oven and let cool about an hour
before topping with the caramel sauce and toffee bits. Refrigerate pie for 4 hours after topping. Serves 8.

*Marion and her daughters love to cook and bake.
She likes to change recipes and make up recipes so she
says entering the Arizona State Fair's different categories has been "music to my soul". She has thoroughly
enjoyed the Crisco American Pie Competition since it
began in 1986. In the 1986 Crisco Pie Competition she
won 1st place in Arizona earning her a chance to compete
in the national competition. She also won first place in
1991 and 1992. Marion's mother taught her well and
she is doing the same for her children and grandchildren. At the age of 8 and 9 her grandchildren are
winning blue ribbons in their county fair in California
where they live.*

Quince Tart

Stanley Rulapaugh — Phoenix

Crust

1 3/4 cup sifted flour
1/2 cup butter (1 stick)
1 egg yolk, slightly beaten
2 Tbsp. ice water

2 Tbsp. sugar
1 Tbsp. lemon juice
1/4 tsp. salt

Cut the butter into small pieces and add to the flour a little at a time, until the mixture resembles coarse meal. Add the beaten egg yolk, ice water, sugar, lemon juice and salt. Work the dough into a mass with your hands. Form into a ball and refrigerate at least two (2) hours.

Quince Filling

6 large, ripe quince
5 cups water
2 1/2 cups sugar
1 cup water
3/4 cup sherry

1 tsp. cinnamon
1/2 tsp. nutmeg
1/2 tsp. salt
2 Tbsp. grated orange peel

Peel and core the quince and immediately place in water to prevent discoloration. Shred the quince using large shredder. Place quince in the 5 cups of water and cook over medium heat about 20 minutes until quince softens. Stir occasionally.

While the quince is cooking, add the sugar to the cup of water and boil until the syrup is clear. Drain the softened quince through a strainer, reserving the liquid. Return quince to pan, add the sugar syrup, sherry, balance of ingredients and 3/4 cup of the reserved liquid. Reheat and reduce liquid until most is gone.

Tart construction: Roll out the chilled crust to about 1/8" thick. Using 4" tart pans, cover the bottoms and sides of each with the crust, pushing the crust into the corners of the pans.

Preheat oven to 350°. Strain quince, reserving liquid. Fill each tart pan with quince filling and enough of the reserved liquid to top of crust. Place tarts in 350° oven for 20 to 25 minutes until crust is golden brown. Serve tarts at room temperature with whipped cream.

INDEX

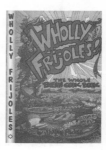

ORDER BLANK

GOLDEN WEST PUBLISHERS

 4113 N. Longview Ave. • Phoenix, AZ 85014

602-265-4392 • **1-800-658-5830** • FAX 602-279-6901

Qty	Title	Price	Amount
	Apple-Lovers Cook Book	6.95	
	Arizona Cook Book	5.95	
	Arizona Small Game Recipes	5.95	
	Arizona State Fair Blue Ribbon Recipes	10.00	
	Best Barbecue Recipes	5.95	
	Chili-Lovers' Cook Book	5.95	
	Chip and Dip Lovers Cook Book	5.95	
	Christmas in Arizona	8.95	
	Cowboy Cartoon Cook Book	5.95	
	Date Recipes	6.95	
	Joy of Muffins	5.95	
	Pecan Lovers Cook Book	6.95	
	Pumpkin Lovers Cook Book	6.95	
	Quick-n-Easy Mexican Recipes	5.95	
	Real New Mexico Chile	6.95	
	Salsa Lovers Cook Book	5.95	
	Sedona Cook Book	7.95	
	Tortilla Lovers Cook Book	6.95	
	What's Cookin' in Arizona!	9.95	
	Wholly Frijoles! The Whole Bean Cook Book	6.95	

Shipping & Handling Add ⮕ U.S. & Canada $2.00
Other countries $5.00

☐ My Check or Money Order Enclosed $

☐ MasterCard ☐ VISA ($20 credit card minimum)

(Payable in U.S. funds)

Acct. No.   Exp. Date

Signature

Name   Telephone

Address

City/State/Zip

10/96

Call for FREE catalog

Blue Ribbon

This order blank may be photo-copied.